Rishabhayan

Rishabhayan

The Story of the First King

ACHARYA MAHAPRAGYA

Translated by
Sudhamahi Regunathan

Foreword by Shivraj V. Patil

HarperCollins *Publishers* India

First published in India in 2015 by Harper Element
An imprint of HarperCollins *Publishers*
4th Floor, Tower A, Building No. 10, Phase II,
DLF Cyber City, Gurugram, Haryana -122002
www.harpercollins.co.in

This edition published in India in 2020 by HarperCollins India

1 2 3 4 5 6 7 8 9 10

P-ISBN: 978-93-5116-007-6
E-ISBN: 978-93-5116-008-3

Typeset in 12/15 Garamond by
R. Ajith Kumar

Printed and bound in India by
Manipal Technologies Limited, Manipal

To the One who is without end, is of ever-flowing wisdom, eternal, and whose abode is eternal

To the One who is engrossed in the soul and the supreme teacher, the first Tirthankara Rishabha

I offer my salutations

To the One who was single-minded in penance and compassionate to his kith and kin. In his family was born Emperor Marichi Kumar who was reborn as the last Tirthankara Mahavira

Those people are worthy of obeisance who strove to advocate human effort and purity of the soul

In this line comes Acharya Bhikshu—may his fame spread

Contents

FAMILY TREE OF THE KULKARS OR CHIEFTAINS

Vimlavahan and twin Chandrayasha

↓

Chakshuman and twin Chandrakanta

↓

Yashasvi and twin Surupa

↓

Abhichandra and twin Pratirupa

↓

Prasenajit and twin Chaksushkrta

↓

Marudev and twin Srikanta

↓

Naabhi and twin Marudev

↓

Rishabha and twin Sumangala

The first King Rishabha

Sumangala ↓ Bharata and Brahmi

Sunanda ↓ Bahubali, Sundari and ninety-nine pairs of twins, plus adopted sons Nami and Vinami

AUTHOR'S NOTE

The story of Rishabha is the story of the beginnings of Indian civilization. History rests on limiting shores; in the mystery of prehistoric times many universes lie hidden.

On the foothills of the Himalayas, a civilization was being born. The Twin Age, or the primitive period, was coming to an end. From dwelling on trees, man was coming down to till the earth to make a living. At that time, in Chieftain Naabhi's house, Rishabha was born. His birth heralded a completely new culture and tradition. His contributions to social organization were so significant that it later made Acharya Jinsen invoke him as the Creator, the one who Bestows, the Maker.

This poem presents the life of Rishabha and so is titled 'Rishabhayan'. The story of Rishabha's life is the biography of social organization. At the crossroads of two time periods the changes that take place in the geographic, social, mental and emotional states make for interesting understanding of the foundation of social development.

Development follows a certain order. Sometimes the order is transgressed and sometimes it is changed. When the order is broken, a leap is taken in progress and when there is a change, it results in a transition. This kind of transition is also called a revolution. It is revolution that transformed the inactivity in The Age of the Twins into Karmayuga. It is revolution that organized wanderers into a kingdom as subjects of King Rishabha.

A healthy society is one in which there is no shortage of wealth and material and yet their influence on people is also not overbearing. In the Age of the Twins, the basic necessities were met but material needs did not wield great influence. Times changed, shortages crept in. When it became difficult to fulfil the needs of life, attachments began to sprout. Soon power began to manifest itself. Life became disorganized. When there is paucity, exploitation, subjugation, intolerance or quarrels, then the need for organization is felt. This situation gave rise to the need for chieftains as leaders and, for a long time, the chieftains or Kulkars ruled organizing society into a structure.

However, the problem of paucity kept growing. It became increasingly difficult to fulfil one's basic needs from the Kalpavriksha alone. The twin problems of power and attachment increased. Twin pairs started exercising authority over all trees. On studying closely both human nature and its inclinations, it seems that paucity acts as an impetus to the growth of feelings of ownership and possession. They are the very same traits of attachment and desire that destroyed the organization under the small chieftains. In order to find a solution to the problem, Chief Naabhi established a kingdom and anointed Rishabha as the first king. The foremost task of the king and his ministers was to make available, and equitably so, the basic necessities of life. In the absence of equitable distribution, crimes increase. When wealth is managed equitably, then the desire to commit crimes reduces.

The kingdom of Rishabha was under the influence of the Age of Twins. At that time the feelings of attachment and power were still sprouting, so while there were occasional incidents of theft and robbery, no major offence ever took place and there was yet no criminal in society. In a way Rishabha was a king of a society that was not used to being ruled over. Material goods were few and so the people were largely free of the desire to possess. Also, self-discipline was the order of the day. Familial relationships were just beginning to be formed and understood, so even on that front, the bonds were not yet very strong. No one had imagined the existence of servants or slaves and so every human being had a strong sense of self-worth. There was no conflict of interests between people and there was an ease in their interaction, which was free of doubt and suspicion of the other. Minimal, clean and natural food was consumed and man's mind and body were largely free of disease and violence. From the modern perspective we could say that since there was not much variety of goods available, the society that Rishabha became king over could be considered underdeveloped. But the mind and thoughts had evolved, so in that sense it was a highly developed society.

Education through learning or teaching had not yet started but discerning perception had been cultivated in great measure. Bhagwan Rishabha taught the people the use of raw materials and how to develop their skills. But after institutionalizing the affairs of the state, he left it all in the quest for his soul. He became a monk and did penance for many days before he was enlightened and could perceive the soul. Since then he became an advocate of the soul. He was the first one of this era to not just experience the soul but also tell the world about it.

The epic presented here has glimpses into many fundamentals of development as well as historical events of the time. These verses were born out of a special imagination—not only for academic research or for people's recitation. Some years ago Gurudev Tulsi had told me, 'Write a poem on Rishabha. It should not be just poetry but also instructional for the soul. It should not be just instructional for the soul, it should also be poetry.' To capture that was not easy, but I have never believed any of my Acharya's suggestions to be difficult and so I set forth. The simplicity of the story gives the experience of a sermon and the rich variations in the moods lend the experience of poetry. The words give the pleasure of a sermon while the suggestions and nuances offer the delicacy of poetry.

In the year 1990, during the chaturmas in Pali, this poem began to take shape. It was completed in Ladnun in the year 1995. Work on it was dictated by routine. To edit the *Agamas* was the primary job at hand. This would go on in the afternoon. The early mornings would be spent in reading and meditation followed by addressing the people in pravachan. Some time would be spent deliberating over the progress and problems of the community. The time for writing 'Rishabhayan' was after dinner and before sunset. Sometimes there would be half an hour available, sometimes twenty minutes. I liked keeping that time for myself, to be in solitude, but often someone would come to discuss a matter that was necessary and my time would get cut into. Our stay in Delhi in the year 1994 went by with practically no work. Sometimes two verses would get written, sometimes one and sometimes three or four. In one way it can be said that this poem came into being in a mechanical fashion. Poetry cannot be mechanical. Only when emotions and the imagination arise can poetry be composed. My situation, however, had been different. Yet the poem was completed. The reason for this was Acharya Tulsi's desire and inspiration. I deem it my good fortune that I was able to complete the poem and present it to him. I was fortunate to see Gurudev's joy also. With Gurudev, I wish I could have deliberated on the poem. That desire remains unfulfilled. In this world of creation-destruction-permanence, to visualize the satisfaction of every desire is by itself an excess.

The great pride of our fold, Muni Madhukarji, transcribed the poem. Jain Vishwa Bharati published it. Muni Dulharaj and

Muni Dhananjay Kumar worked hard to edit and clean it up. Now, after a short period of waiting, it is being made available to the reader.

1 December 1999

Acharya Mahapragya
Adhyatma Sadhna Kendra
Mehrauli, New Delhi

Translator's Note

An imagery I associate with making an offering is to cup the hands and gently let the front of the fingers fall so that the cupped palms can pour water or shower flowers, depending on what they hold. The mudra of cupped palms is called pushpaputam. My cupped palms hold words made from Roman alphabets. As they tumble down at the feet of Acharya Mahapragya, they come together as the translation of his composition, the 'Rishabhayan'.

I wandered into 'Rishabhayan' quite by chance. I had translated many collections of poems by Acharyashree and was looking for more verse by him when I came across this epic, which began with the belying simple verse:

Water exists, snow exists
Water the source, snow its form
Wind exists, water exists
Wind the source, water its form

It was exciting for me to see more than 2,000 verses awaiting translation into English and I jumped into it with the confidence of the ignorant. Unknowing of what awaited me, I declared to Acharyashree that I had begun the translation of 'Rishabhayan'. He was, I think, a little surprised and a lot delighted. 'Achcha?' he said, half in question, half in exclamation.

Holding on to that twinkle in his eye and that delight which he seemed to feel, I embarked on my self-assigned project with great gusto. What I thought would be a search for words with similar meanings turned out to be a search all right, but for the very warp and weft which holds the words, for the grid that sustains life, for an understanding that is yet elusive.

Rishabhayan is composed in 2,000 verses. The original is in Hindi with liberal usage of Sanskrit and Rajasthani words, aphorisms and metaphors. The mythological story of Rishabha, the first Tirthankara or the first ford-maker, is told with special emphasis on the philosophy and teachings that came with it. It was a challenge not only to find the equivalents of philosophical terms but also to capture the symbolism of certain terms which far overreach their literal meaning. And yet it was important to keep to the literal because Acharya Mahapragya chose his words with care. They allow for myriad understandings and perspectives. Further, his style of writing is such that part of the story is told and part is left to be understood in the gaps between the words. Acharya Mahapragya believed in brevity and all his writings are at first glance enigmatic, and on closer look so full of meaning that an essay can be written on just a short sentence. His sentences are short and his style direct. I have also observed that he only suggests, and never forces his view point. He may assert his belief, but his language is conscious of relativity even in expression. He treads on ideas and counter ideas with the sensitivity of a classic Jain monk in the pursuit of non-violence. An example would be his manner of sentence construction. One finds he uses the passive voice very often. I have tried to retain that because even if the sentence does not read smoothly in English, there comes about a subtle change in meaning if one changes it to the active voice.

Our concern—and now I talk as a reader—is with what he is trying to convey, to allow for a discussion along the lines of 'Does he mean it this way or that...?', to be able to use words only as the sketch and fill in the colour ourselves with the spirit that overrides the writing. I have always believed I am translating, if I may coin a new word—'non-expression'—in his communications, rather than the words themselves. Between one full stop and the next sentence, a kingdom can be built. And yet one sentence follows another. My attempt has been to retain this relation between space and continuity.

I have had to refer to some texts (as mentioned in the notes) in order to understand the meaning and import of some names and incidents. This understanding of mine I have tried to present in short storylines at the beginning of every canto to provide for a better understanding in a new language, and to bridge the transition from one thought to another. In most places

I have been very loyal to the original. In some I have had to give the intended meaning as I understood it. The concern to keep it in meter, and thus short, helped to decide the approach. All through, I have tried to keep the meter as in the original. I cannot begin to reflect on my good fortune that led me to this translation or, in fact, to Acharyashree. Acharyashree had once said that once I finish translating 'Rishabhayan', I would be a changed person. While that is true, what remains truer is Acharyashree's influence on my mind and aspirations.

It has taken me a long time to bring the manuscript to this level, about three-and-a-half to four years. This period has seen as many lows as highs. The first blow came when Acharyashree left his body on the 9th of May of 2009. He was a month short of ninety. My main motivation to finish the task I had undertaken was to present it to him. That desire was left unfulfilled. Many months later, when I was translating the preface, I found a similar sentiment expressed by him where he says he finished his writing of the 'Rishabhayan' inspired by his guru Acharya Tulsi, but life did not give him adequate time to sit and discuss it with him. I had shown Acharya Mahapragya the cantos I had finished, but I had barely reached Canto IX then.

Somehow, after the May of 2009, the translation moved faster. Irrational as it may sound, I felt his presence with me and my understanding far surpassed my intellect. Even to that, however, there were limits. One day I was very depressed, ruing my foolishness at undertaking something for which I was not equipped. At that time I looked for help. I was very choosy about the kind of help I wanted. I did not want anyone to touch my words or abet my understanding. I was translating 'Rishabhayan' as per my understanding, not just of the words written by Acharyaji but also of him as I knew him. The struggle has been to capture the silence in his words, the elegance in his thought and the beauty in the vision his eyes saw. Some part of my effort should turn out right and that should serve as the foundation for further explorations. That I was certain of.

I wanted help to understand some Jain philosophical and mythological concepts. I do not ascribe it to chance that I heard Muni Jaykumar was at that time in Delhi and that too in the area where I live. Muni Jaykumar is one who has been serving Acharyashree for many years and also during the period of the composition of 'Rishabhayan'. He is a poet himself and so understands that which is unsaid. My access to him was made as easy as possible and the couple of months that I visited him have added invaluable merit to the work. My gratitude to him transcends the feeling.

The translation was challenging not only because I had to find synonyms for philosophical terms, but also because I had to accommodate adages and proverbs that are common in Hindi, Rajasthani and Sanskrit in a culturally different language. So, while in some places I have been able to find literal equivalents which also retain the flavour and meaning of the original, in others I have had to present the meaning as I understand it. In the punctuation, too, I have kept to the spirit of the original.

There have been many members of the community who have

helped me at different stages, from making available reference books to helping me meet Muniji. I salute the entire community for its help.

The benign and understanding smile of Acharya Mahashraman makes me feel he understands what I miss and what I enjoy. So too with Sadhvi Pramukhashree, whose silent communication is eloquent. I think of Sadhvi Vishrut Vibha as a sahrdya. Muni Kishanlal was the one who introduced us to Acharyashree.

Once, in my role as Vice-Chancellor, I had gone to Acharya Mahapragya, the spiritual guide to the university, with a problem. 'Surendran will help you,' he said confidently and instructed his devotees that my meeting with him be organized. I met a soft-spoken gentleman who had won the confidence of Acharyashree as a man who could accomplish not just the most difficult of tasks but could also take the people along with him. But for him, Mr Surendran Chauraria, this manuscript would not have reached the publisher's desk.

Every manuscript comes with its own destiny and so it was that it met Mr Krishan Chopra at HarperCollins. His understanding of the importance of Acharya Mahapragya's work was instrumental in its acceptance for publication.

On reaching there, it was the play of providence again that brought a sensitive editor to the table. Ms Debasri Rakshit has been patient and very discriminating in her suggestions. I will miss interacting with her once the editing is over.

In Acharyaji's play *Ashruveena*, the following line occurs in one verse:

Sandehanam jhatiti vasatirlangneeyantarapta
If en route you happen to pass by the city of doubt,
cross it with one long leap, as fast as you can

Even though I had the verse inscribed on every corner of my

work table, the meaning often got lost on me and there were three people who took me back to it. Dr Rajan has been a constant source of encouragement to the extent that I have wondered if it was only his devotion to Acharyashree that made him see my work in a good light, or if there was really any merit in it, any purpose behind it.

Either way, he was convincing enough in the moments of angst, and I moved on.

I had and have another pillar of support, Mr M.L. Sethia. That he bought me beautiful Hindi dictionaries is a fact that pales in front of the conviction he had that I was indeed doing something no one else could do! Such blind belief, even if one knows is subjectively inspired, makes for good feeling.

Acharya Mahapragya referred to Dr Rajan, Mr Sethia, my husband S. Regunathan and me as the four pillars of the four-sided figure, the chatushkon, and he went further on to emphasize its significance. Without the tolerance and patience of the third pillar, whose vow to stand by me through thick and thin was truly put to test, nothing could have happened. It was, in fact, my husband who introduced me to Acharyashree, and Acharyashree constantly reminded me that my husband was known to him before he knew me. Acharyashree, in person and now in memory, continues to add glow to our life together... Above all, I owe much to my mother.

30 October 2014 Sudhamahi Regunathan

Foreword

Rishabhayan is a story told in about 2,000 verses about the first Tirthankara of the Jain religion, Rishabha or Adinatha.

Jain mythology believes it was the birth of Rishabha that heralded the organization of society, the development of its administration, the origin of vocational skills, education, and the beginning of social institutions like the family and the relationships born thereof. Therefore, the story of Rishabha is not just a portrait of the period before the manifestation of the above features, but also a description of how they came to be. In that process the ideal society, the desirable administrative impulses so as to ensure equitable distribution of wealth, the purpose and importance of education of both men and women and the human character of rectitude have been sketched with detail and enthusiasm in the verses of Rishabhayan.

Acharya Mahapragya, a prolific writer (with over 200 books in every genre: play, prose writing, philosophical discourse and poetry), understood the elements that go in the making of a story. In this epic poem, where each verse is generally of four lines each and some (around fifty of them) of six lines, Acharya Mahapragya tells the story of Rishabha along with the story of the genesis of Jain thought. All the navarasas or nine emotions play out to build a tale of personal aggression, ambition, the rage of war, the pain of separation and the birth of philosophy.

Acharya Mahapragya has showcased his poetic sensibility and his ascetic sensibility in this work. My association with him has always been intellectually rewarding for he was a man whose clarity made his expression sparkle with both contemporary relevance and satiric wit. While going through this work, I felt I was sitting beside him, listening to his rendition of Jain mythology. He wrote with enthusiasm and devotion, but all the while remembering the fundamental Jain principle of anekanta. This brought restraint to his expressions and that remains their greatest charm.

The contribution of the Jains to ancient Indian literature, both in Sanskrit and Prakrit, has been immense. One of the characteristics of their work is the delineation, in detail, of all the vices which should be avoided and the pursuance of which will be detrimental, with this lesson: the hero or heroine will eventually turn towards total renunciation or monkhood. The pattern originates with the story of Rishabha who was king. He had a hundred plus one sons. He divided his kingdom between them all after a certain point in time, and himself took to introspection after complete renunciation. It was then that he enunciated the fundamental principles of Jainism, namely, that the body and soul are different. That the body is just matter, and that in matter the three activities of origination, destruction and permanence coexist simultaneously. The soul, he said further, is similar in all living beings and everyone shares the desire to live. It is this thought that took the shape of non-violence, and non-possession and non-absolutism came as pillars on which non-violence could rest.

Meanwhile, his sons were enjoying their kingdoms when his eldest son, Bharata, wanted to annexe all his brothers' kingdoms. Ninety-nine of them gave in to him without a fight. How did they do that? What motivated them? The repercussions of their actions are still being experienced by us . . . They all opted for the kingdom which no one could take away from them: the kingdom of the soul. They renounced all worldly attachments. This is the first instance of a sangha being formed, and even today the Jain ascetics remain a strong group.

Bharata and Bahubali engaged in war for neither could give up so easily. What would the outcome be? Most readers will recognize their mental turmoil as they are separated from us only in time and not in nature.

The first canto talks of the times before the birth of Rishabha, followed by his birth, the establishment of kingdoms and the creation of society. Canto V is about Bharata being crowned king. In Canto VI, the initiation of Rishabha into monkhood is described and the following canto is about the festival of Akshay Tritiya, which is the day when Rishabha receives alms for the first time after many years of fasting and penance. In Canto VII, Rishabha's realization is described and the following canto gives the essence of his teachings. Three cantos after this describe Bharata's conquests. The remaining are about the war between Bharata and his brothers and the final outcome. Rishabhayan ends with Rishabha attaining nirvana.

I am happy Rishabhayan has been translated into the English and that too kept in verse as it is in the original. I am happy to read the same flow of poetry in the English as it was in the Hindi. I am sure more people will benefit from this translation, both from Acharya Mahapragya's scholarship and in understanding Jain mythology.

10 November 2014 Shivraj V. Patil

Canto I

Every story is set in its own specific time and space and couched within the metaphors of its creators. Rishabhayan is the story of Rishabha, the first Tirthankara in the Jain tradition and told by a Jain Acharya. The poem begins with addressing the eternal question of how we came to be. Who made these mountains and the rivers running by? Who made our life and designed it so? Who made the birds that sing and the sun that shines? The search for an answer to these questions has also come to be known as the search for truth. Truth being elusive, the search continues and is continually enhanced by many schools of thought thus giving birth to philosophy and religion.

The Jain version of the story begins with the declaration that the story of our universe has neither a beginning nor an end. It does not even have a creator. According to Jain philosophy, there are six astikayas or states of matter which are made of a collection of molecules of the same state. They are: dharma-astikaya which supports motion, adharma astikaya which is the medium of rest, akash astikaya which provides accommodation, pudgal astikaya or matter which has attributes of colour, smell, taste and touch, kal astikaya, which is time, and jiva or the animate. That is what is referred to in 'The causal collection of molecules.'

Jiva (animate) and ajiva (inanimate) is another important distinction in Jainism and so the word has been retained in the poem. Jiva literally means 'living being', 'principle of life'.[i] However, the implicit sense in which jiva is understood in Jain philosophy is of being the soul. Ajiva is the inanimate principle. It does not have consciousness and cannot accumulate karmas. Dharma astikaya, adharma astikaya, akasha astikaya, pudgala astikaya and kal are categorized as ajiva.

The division between the jiva and the ajiva states is clear and there can be no movement from the ajiva state to the jiva. However, within the jiva state, on the basis of how pure and evolved the soul is, human life is said to exist in four states: naraki or those who live in hell, tiryancha or the animals, plants and similar beings, manushya or human beings, and deva or heavenly beings or those who access a better life full of luxuries and comfort and occupy the highest rung in the ladder of existence. The soul is reborn in one of the four categories depending on one's karma.

The fourth verse of the first canto, which talks of the motion in the leaves and the flapping wings of the birds in contrast to the state of rest of the tree trunk, refers to the first two astikayas (dharma and adharma). The seat of the birds refers to the idea of akshastikaya or that which provides accommodation. The fifth verse talks of time and that all changes that we see in this world are wrought by time. There is discussion in quite some length about why time, which cannot be broken down into atoms, is considered to be a basic state of matter. The reason given by Swetambar Jains is illustrated by Acharya Mahapragya in the verse where he says time enables transformation of not just matter into different forms called 'modes' or paryaya but also maintains the continuity of the soul which is eternal through finding different

---

[i]Monier Williams, *Sanskrit English Dictionary*, 1899: 422.

bodies as houses. Therefore since it helps in the activity of life, it is considered a basic state of matter.

The story we are about to read is set in the time period known as Sushma-Sushma.

Time, as we have seen above, is expressive of creation and destruction. This cycle of time thus follows two phases: Avasarpini, in which the destructive process is on and Utsarpini, in which the constructive forces are in action. Each of the phases have within them six divisions which are Sushma-Sushma, Sushma, Sushma-Dushma, Dushma-Sushma, Dushma and, finally, Dushma-Dushma. This is the order in which they occur in the Avasarpini phase, where Sushma is the progressive and prosperous phase while Dushma is the regressive and destructive phase. For Utsarpini the order is reversed. The story recounted begins with the first stage of the Avasarpini phase which is Sushma-Sushma (it is believed we are currently in the Dushma phase).

There is a mention that people in the time of Sushma-Sushma used to live till infinity. That means they should still be around. The word used is palya, which is a measure of time. Palya is a period which cannot be measured. But if you wish to measure, the method is given in the Jain texts: a well four kos wide and deep. Fill that well with the hair of newly born twins. The infant's hair is 1/2401 part of the width of an adult's hair. This hair has to be broken into tiny bits and the well is to be filled with them. Every hundred years, if one small piece of hair is removed from the well, then the time taken to clear the well is one palya.[ii]

The poem begins with the words 'salil satya hai'. Salil would normally translate as truth, but in this context it means that even though water exists and snow also exists, they are but two forms of the same entity. This first section is a concise exposition of the

---

[ii] Acharya Mahapragya, *Jain Darshan, Manan aur Mimamsa*, Adarsh Sahitya Sangh, 1995.

concept of anekanta or relativity which forms the basis of Jain philosophy. It says, in Acharya Mahapragya's words, 'As many as there are, their count will remain the same, the change of form is called transience.' In other words, this is the Jain derivation of the theory that matter can neither be created nor destroyed. The multiplicity of the things around us is a result of a change in their 'mode' or appearance, just like snow and water. In every element, there are three aspects of origination, destruction and permanence, which lead us to the thought that the seed of all possibilities exist in a thing. So in the infant itself youth and old age are waiting to be manifest. That is why Acharya Mahapragya defines anekanta also as the coexistence of opposites. Truth and untruth, he says, are partners.

Throughout Canto I, Acharya Mahapragya refers to anekanta off and on. Anekanta or relativity of truth has been not just Acharya Mahapragya's theme for his books but also his life.

Going back to the story, we may say that once upon a time, in the period of Sushma-Sushma, there were few people on earth and they lived each for his own; they were not organized into a community or village or any such group. They were born as pairs and the pairs also mated with each other to bring forth yet another pair. Obviously, even then relationships like father and mother, brother and sister did exist but they were not bound by emotions. Life was quite simple. No one had to work for a living. Food was available in plenty and the people consumed food maybe once in three days and that too tiny portions.

All requirements were met by trees known as the Kalpavrikshas. Mythologically, the Kalpavriksha was believed to be the wish-fulfilling tree which could grant a person any object that he wished for. Ten types of trees meeting ten different needs have been mentioned in the *Tanam* (section 10, sutra 142) and they have been described in the canto.

Now this blissful period gave way to the next which was Sushma and later Sushma-Dushma, one worse than the other. The whole story began with paucity. The Kalpavriksha was unable to meet the requirements of the people. So, as Acharya Mahapragya says, the desire to posses, greed and avarice came into existence. A leader was required who could organize the available material for equitable distribution. These leaders came to be known as the Kulkars or chieftains. There were seven of them: Vimlavahan and his wife Chandrayasha, Chakshuman and his wife Chandrakanta, Yashasvi and his wife Surupa, Abhichandra and his wife Pratirupa, Prasenajit and his wife Chaksushkrta, Marudev and his wife Srikanta, and Naabhi and his wife Marudev (*Tanam*, section 7, sutra 63.).

The art of administration was born. Punishment was the first tool. Initially remorse, hakar as it was called, was enough to control people. Soon they grew thick-skinned and one had to be a little more eloquent and direct admonishment was used. Not for too long was crime contained by admonishment alone and 'man wore the skin of punishment closer'. The third tool was dhikkar or reprimand.

The canto ends with Naabhi, the last Kulkar, seeing a new future in meditation. A new order had to come to be—how much punishment can you impose, how many controls can you institute? Sometimes a whole new thought process is required to transform society.

Water exists, snow exists
Water the source, snow its form
Wind exists, water exists
Wind the source, water its form

Wind, water, snow—existential truths[1] are
Their atoms infinite and without beginning
Animal-human-heavenly being,[2] a cycle of changing forms
The soul, the source, of no end or beginning

Truth and untruth are partners
No exception to the rule
Rain is born of the cloud and that is destiny's script
Who can change it, whose opinion counts?

Every branch, every leaf is
the seat of birds with flapping wings
The base unmoving, the fluttering leaves
Both together part of one single tree

Existence is not beyond time, nor
does it the past or future contain
It is the transformation wrought by time that turns
milk into ghee for oblation

Truth, untruth are words relative
No exception to this rule
In the infant, the youth, the youthful
Adult and a glimpse of old age are contained

Sentience and insentience, the two
are the only truths eternal
As many there are, their count will remain
The change of form is called the transience

The consuming sentient, the consumed insentient[3]
Filled with the two is the world
'Was', 'is', 'will be', in the courtyard
of these words, no sorrow of death will be

The world and its creation

The play of the sentient and the insentient
Creates the world's variety, the birth of synonyms[4]
The eternal world, the enactment of creation
Is carried forth with collective efficiency

The causal collection of molecules[5]
Self-generating, timeless and infinite
Varied forms, diverse transformations
Autumn, cyclones and spring

Spread across sky-space, the atoms
Together make a collective entity
From which the jiva its body makes
And the golden form its brilliance attains

The jiva gets form anew with the body
So vast is the world of manifestations
Either infused with jiva or without
Is every branch on the tree

Earth, water, fire, air,
Plants—are all bodies imbued with jiva
Engulfed by matter all living beings are
As water is bound by the shores

In the theatre of life, these two actors,
Jiva and ajiva, are playing different games
Because of their varied modes and manifestations
Green and flourishing is the tree of life

Matter, resplendent, comes together with the jiva
and life is infused within it
And through that every activity
Of the sentient being is carried forth

The subtle transforms into the gross
And the gross then returns to the subtle
Unimaginable are the myriad transformations
Knowledge insentient, sentient the knower

India

In the incomparable limitless space
The sky is but a small dot
With the rays of the infinite particles of dawn
Cast wide is the net of light

Countless islands on this earth
One land mass is our blessed India
Cleansed, awash with light and brilliance
Of the mighty snow-clad peaks of the Himalayas

The cycle of time

The cause of change is time
Which flows like a water stream
This cycle of time of twelve periods
Is always on the move

In the age of Avasarpini[6]
Matter is systematically destroyed
In the age of Utsarpini[7]
Matter is systematically built

The Age of Twins

In the first phase of Sushma[8]
People were few but always happy
There was no problem of overpopulation
And nature brought forth new life in pairs

There was no village, no city
In the forests lived everyone
No houses there, nor kitchens to cook
Living naturally like ascetics

No kingdom, nor any society
Each one to his own
And so this society existed
Without any governance

Anger appeased, arrogance quietened
Illusion and greed unseen
Without governance, society flourishes
When the grip of emotions is light

In such a state
People are not motivated
Only the desire-less and detached
can take such a society forward

The mind of a dictator
Rules by suppressing
With spiritual discipline
Comes the rise of divinity

No wealth there was, nor punishment
Not required was any trade
Limited needs, limited desires
Life itself, in a sense, limited

The requirements of life
Were all fulfilled by the wish-fulfilling tree[9]
No disease was there, nor treatment
Not even available was the triphala churan[10]

Free is the one who wanders as per wish
Dependent is the one who in a community lives
Gold, silver, gems and pearls were all to be found
But their consumption was still to grow

Master-servant relationship non-existent was
Nor felt was the need for service
No expectation was there of greatness
Self-reliant was each and every one

Mother-father, brother-sister
Was the family relationship
But unfettered was their lifestyle
Not passionate in the bonds of love

Those who were friends, companions
Not bound by passion either
Not one was a sworn enemy
The regret of enmity was unknown

Drama, dance, music were unborn
Content was the mind without amusement
Elephants, goats, cows there were
But man-animal relationship was still unformed

Not violent was the lion or leopard
Appearance gentle, nature peaceful
Mosquito and bugs did not frequent
the earth, which was pest free

Sure enough python, snake and other reptiles
lived, but engrossed they were in themselves
Of each other fearless and easily accepting
Growing and flourishing at their own pace and ways

Conflict, fights, aggression not there
Weapons had not been made
As though on this sacred earth
Was established liberation anew

Wish-fulfilling tree[11]

From Chitra came the food
Which formed the basis of life
The giver of garment was the tree Anagn
Covering nudity with its bark

Leaves of Mrig served as containers
And the Gohakar served as home for forest dwellers
Jyotishang heat radiated
And the Maniang gave gem-like ornaments

Lamp-like Dipang spread light
Instrumental music resonated from the Trutitang
The Chitrang gave a garland of varied flowers
For Nectar-like headiness, the source was the Madang

Food

Much sweeter than sugar
Was the dust of the earth
Its sweetness even in
the river water was to be found

Nutritive elements in doses small
Food itself in quantities mean
Only every third day
Came the desire to eat a meal

Strong bones with joints of Vajrarishabhanarach[12]
The hearts of people were pure and clear
They lived into infinity
Indeed a lifespan beyond logic

Lack of anger, lack of greed,
Mental peace, positive outlook, and
Balanced nutrition, these five potent
influences ensured longevity

The causes of a short lifespan are five:
Fear, stress, passions high,
Imbalanced food and the collective effect
Of all negative emotions and thoughts

Free were the twins from all of these
Brief was the product range for consumption
So there was elegance in conduct
Nowhere any deception or malintent

Dharma and a calm mind
A healthy body, all part of a natural flow
Great was this wondrous period
As all the twins were of one mind

With the power of being in the flow
Present-day life was holy, so was afterlife
On death the twins were ensured
Of their singular destination: heaven[13]

Reading, learning, language, poetry
Science or even logic
Everything was concealed just as
The stars are in bright daylight

No actor, no script
Natural environment
By nature in contentment
As though the heavens had descended there

Life in the flow, death too
Through chittasamadhi[14]
Nobody ever died due to
Illness—physical, mental or emotional

Giving birth to the next pair
Short was their life after that
In silence unfolding
The story of the pair

The seven-day-old infant sleeping on
his back, would be sucking his thumb
And in the second week, on the strength
of his knees, would crawl without support

Speech forming, walking wobbly
Would slowly gain strength in his legs
Developing motor skills by the seventh week
A young man he would be

For nourishment till the forty-ninth day
He would to his parents be indebted
And then would just take wing as with a sneeze
or yawn, the bird flies away spreading its wings

On the strength of his effort
Would live the youth
One's own lamp, one's own wick oiled
Glowing through the strength of one's own light

The cause of change is time
Everyone is governed by time
No one ever remains the same
So the enlightened ones have said

As the chariot of time rolled on
So moved the cycle of destruction
In the journey of progress and regress, sometimes
it is easy to get milk, tougher to get whey

The wheels of change

With the changes in the solar cycle
The age also undergoes change,
In Sushma period there was sweet delicacy
In food intake every third day

Between Sushma and Dushma
Small problems came to fore
The one source of all food, the Kalpataru[15]
Was not every thirst able to quench

In the Dushma-Sushma period
The dark night came to prominence
This complicated cycle of day and night
Who has been able to understand it?

In the Kalpavriksha's[16] capabilities
There came much miserliness
Lightning struck it and twin
pairs fumbled in distress and chaos

It is true of difficult times that
When an untoward event takes place
The existent consciousness becomes dormant
While the dormant consciousness awakens anew

Those who had always been free of affection
Rose in them a surge of possessiveness
Each one of them now began
to assert their right over the Kalpavriksha

Robbing, snatching, aggression
Grew all around
As though obsessed they were to
destroy all peace and energy

Is this true? True it is that in paucity
The character gets perverted
But remember the stimulation to progress comes
from immediate and fundamental causes

Relative truth

Acquisition is the principal truth
A unidimensional perspective this
As the circumstances, so the consequences
This is a one-sided view

In milk the inherent pride of butter within
is expressed upon churning it right
The core matter similar, manifestations different
Relativity or the principle of anekanta extant[17]

The stars get hidden by the day
In darkness they get back their light
Fire is present in wood
But without friction it does not manifest

In search of leadership

All around the pairs there were problems
Times seemed to be indeed changing
For the first time came a state of paucity
The script of this story—who wrote?

Growing hunger every day, scarcity of food
Completely unprecedented and unseen
The need today is to find a problem-solver
Desired is a new course of action

People met to discuss with each other
Conferences took place
One thought, one worry
There was only one chapter read

If this time-wrought social problem
Had not sown the seed,
The need for thinking and reflection
Would never have gained momentum

Problems cannot just remain problems
And man cannot but face them straight
In the absence of the heat of fire
The pot of clay does not cook

From difficulties arise
these rays of illumination
Infatuation gives birth to darkness
Intellect, a fallacious picture of the heavens paints

The rise of the Kulkar state

The last few hours of the Sushma-Dushma
period were now drawing to a close
The wandering pairs now very busy
And the sky said what it never had before

A four-tusked elephant, white
as the Himalayas, came forth majestically
Picking up the male twin
with his trunk, seated him on his back

First vehicle, first commuter
Saw everyone a wondrous sight
Every pair moves on its feet,
Now who is this so strong?

Elephants saw, humans also saw
Elephant mounted, unseen so far
A climb of just four steps, but
so far unmatched, unthought of

Elegant vehicle, a beautiful form
So naturally named was he Vimlavahan
The pure-hearted duo
Saw together a new dawn

With the sacred memory of the past
A strong bond between them held
Where is the need for authority
When the hearts are in harmony?

When suddenly someone takes possession
Of the Kalpavriksha that belongs to all
The feeling of having lost out comes first
Followed by possessiveness at heart

Quarrels, fights between them grew
The elephant rider is elder, they thought
Justice all will get from him, the best
he is in intellect, patience and understanding

He will be our chief
Acceptable to us is his advice
The subject-master relationship
From today began to take shape

After lengthy discussions, the twins
In the presence of Vimlavahan came
With new creative energy and new perspective
The wilting flowers bloomed again

Collective prayer

Seated on a mount so high
You are a sight to behold, O Lord!
The stature you have gained is on your own
Without being a follower of anyone

Rule us, O lord, become our chief
This a common desire we share
Our inner faith is certain
That our prayers will be answered

Vimlavahan

Why a common leader for one and all
We each can lead our selves,
If every one his decorum and
self-discipline keeps

Man's intellect is spotless and pure
And in that it is an evolved mind
On the royal route along four states
of existence,[18] man's life is indeed blessed

Twins

Lord, the problem is more difficult
How changed has become our life
Even the Kalpavriksha has changed
And so has human conduct

When one is able to exercise self-discipline
Then a leader is born
He alone can be the one to correct
Those following the wrong path

Vimlavahan

If rules be acceptable and the ruler too
Only then organization can happen
Without a thread how can we string
The garland of the mind?

The concept of ruler and ruled—with both
the twins unacquainted
Under these circumstances, how can anyone
be a leader, tell me brother?

The water that flows from experience
Is water that is invaluable
Truth rippling in its many forms
Is stationary and yet flowing

The situation of the twins will change
Now ruled by their own nature they are
Through the myriad rules and regulations
The form of an organization will come to be

At this time in the change of ages
This will be an experience great
Think, reflect and then tell me:
Does everyone faith in it have?

Having breathed fresh air
Having roamed free under the sky
How will that kind of bird
Love the cage even for a second?

Twins

What you say is right, your thoughts are right
We have lived unbound and free
But defenceless in this chaos we are
Though drunk we have every second, the nectar of peace

Rendered helpless the forest elephant
Has overcoming his ego, accepted authority
Becoming one with the dust of the earth
Is choosing greener pastures of life

The ruler and his rule we will make acceptable
And give it utmost respect
With the comfort of organization, forever
far away from us will be our arrogance

The order of rules, that which are well laid out
That in truth is the real freedom
The one who is fostered in arrogance
Even in independence, enslaved is he

Chanting 'Om Om' from the inner recesses
of your mind, now bless us all
Just as a word on finding meaning
becomes meaningful and of consequence

The third eye is ready to open
And allow the flow of compassion
Tearing through the chest of darkness
We have to emerge anew

Vimlavahan[19]

To guide you all along the right path
My services are ready
We have to grow in partnership
Come, walk to the right and left of me

The whole atmosphere was excited
New sunrise in golden splendour
Appointed as soon as destiny chose a chieftain
Was born the constitution of the new creation

Organizing people into a kul,[20] Vimlavahan
became the chieftain well-known
The first step towards organization was taken
And history came to be made

One citadel of power to begin with
Was like a dewdrop on the grass
With the collection of one drop after another
The unparalleled ocean comes to be

Distribution system

Dividing equally, let us share the produce of the Kalpavriksha
Like the rose flower is fragrant even if the bush has thorns
Let us share and enjoy whatever is available
And understand the principle of beneficial interdependence

The first state of social cohesion in the Age of the Twins
Equal distribution to all, equal status to all
To be partial was unimaginable to the chieftain
Just as to spread light alone is the job of the sun

The beginning of punishment

With great regard did everyone respect the chieftain's rule
The desire to rule is like the allure of magic
Once awakened, the desire is difficult to suppress
And can make even the impossible possible

Gradually the minds of the twins underwent change
There came a frightening gust of greed,
Which sought to wield authority over others' trees
Everything got consumed in this fire of greed

The problem was presented to the chieftain
To obtain a solution requires great penance
Engrossed in meditation, truth emerged
Enforcing discipline is the strongest punitive measure

He saw the gentle-hearted twins
And made the smallest hint of a rule
'What have you done?' these words harsh,
called hakar, would wilt away any attack or unjust act

In this reprimand was the punishment to disobedience
That brought into discipline the minds of every pair
Respect and insult are primarily social concepts
To the lone individual they are notions meaningless

The limitless power of words was accepted
and recognized by society, without any debate
Till now limited was activity and speech well regulated
Everything seen and unseen was full of hope and thirst

Came the end of nature-synchronic life, began the drive of
suppression
Every twin was now threaded into one single garland
Suddenly came this new period of this new age
Like a cloud on a clear blue sky

The end of the Age of Twins

Time is ever moving
Nothing is ever static
The rising tide of the ocean
Is hiding the waves from vision

Even though life was long
A deadline in death was inevitable
Life-giving breath when obstructed within,
means death of the physical being

The ever healthy body
And no disease to it born
Is as rare in the world as
amity in the evil-hearted

Eternal youth, beautiful,
Ageing, an idea unborn
But death invincible
Went together along

A new prospect now opened
A new life in the womb
A source of wonder, no doubt
No surprise then in its flying away[21]

At twilight, Chandrayasha[22]
Gave birth to twins
One was male, the other female
And the order of pairs came to be

The twins grew very fast
By the sixth month they attained youth
Times change, rules change
Sometimes millet, sometimes peas[23]

Six months completed, then
the twins breathed their last
With one sneeze they died naturally
Connected are creation and destruction

Just as for the new leaf
The old one makes space
So too on no one's head has remained
An umbrella of protection forever

Came responsibility
to Chakshuman
A Kulkar he became, as also
The first example of a follower

As work
expands,
So does
vocabulary grow

Celebrate everyone did
Gaining new leadership
In his leadership they saw
A dedication father-like

Lifestyles were similar
Contentment and joy came with the flow
No desire was there for greatness
Natural was the astral body

Balanced progress took place
No new heights were touched
Life duration uncertain
Historical accounts of it, short

The law of Makar

Came a new morning in the Kulkar age
The cycle of day and night as that of the known and unknown
Yashasvi took to succession, as
the intellectual fills himself with joy

As the ascetic blooms lotus-like
With a firm resolve, like the fragrance
from a bed of flowers
reaffirmed by the wind

He set about guarding the twins
As a cowherd would his herd
Everything, everyone filled with
the culture of cooperation and oneness

Just as the intoxicated elephant
Rendered futile any mahout's instructions
The passions of the twins drew its
momentum from the wind

The age was now
overstepping the limits of hakar
So problems came galloping along
The essence lost its being

And all of a sudden, the problems snowballed
And played a song continually
The one who sought answers
Was seeing truth at every step

The truth was that this medicine
would no longer fit the bill
The need is for a change of remedy
to bind the minds of the twins anew

The order of makar was announced
And the Age of Twins moved ahead
From an invisible corner of the horizon
The order came resounding

Crime committed due to scarcity
Was by hakar controlled
When it stepped beyond, admonishments like
'You are forbidden' washed the mind clear of vice

Generally, in correcting mistakes, both
the punishments were used
That was enough reprimand
To lower the eyelids in shame

Suppression would be an alternative
When the man's mind is in slumber deep
The poisonous seed of punishment
Man is sowing with his own hands

The fourth Kulkar Abhichandra
Took both the type of reprimands as base
And administered
Like his father in all grace

The flow of the water then
was smooth and on even ground
But tell me, how can a new morn rise
Without the seed of desire?

The law of Dhikkar

Calm the ocean, calm the waves
Suddenly blew in a storm
The mind and emotions were
incomprehensibly high strung

The wave of violation and excess
Tore the fabric of the organization
Just like the one in rising passion
Gives up his sense of shame

Suppression is easy, difficult is transformation
of the heart: an age-old truth
Bringing about change is but an imagination
Punishment seems like the widely accepted norm

As the net of excesses
Spread wide and far
So man wore closer
The skin of punitive power

To enforce the law of dhikkar
Was the gift of fifth Kulkar Prasenajit
It became the command to control the uncontrolled
Governance still administered by words

Just as the soundless knows sound
As soon as life is breathed into the lifeless
As moisture is required for the drums to produce sound
So too culture required punitive measures to form

Sweetness, harshness became two
genres of words in the vocabulary
Coloured by emotions of love and hate
They became either nectar or venom

The union of language and its intent
Still is a mystery in philosophy
Except that only language which with meaning is infused
Becomes known to the knower

With the support of these three laws
The sutra for administration was founded
That remained the path that Marudev tread
The son has to measure up to the father

Now came the period of Naabhi's reign
His wife Marudev by name
The story of the period of the twins
Was now coming to a full stop

The eternal and the constantly changing, both are truths
The soul and matter, both are truths
In the discipline of anekanta[24]
No difference of opinion could be found

The ocean is calm, it is full of waves
Water and waves both relative
One is eternal, one momentary
Only the basic atom absolute

Only the permanent, only change
is as much of a fantasy as a flower in the sky
Natural is the mud, its form is the pot
The name of multiple variations is development

Humans and man-made organizations
Are all those that undergo change
Answered the question is even today
Whether a particular thing is decent or indecent

Contemporary philosophy, impartial
But not discussed in this world or the other
Mother-father, husband-wife
Brother-sister, daughter-son

These eight relationships
All related to the family
Brother-sister became husband-wife
A contract in relationship accepted by all

The changes wrought by space and time
Move according to the cycle of nature
Grass, from grass to milk, milk to cream
And from cream comes butter

'Even Indra has difficulty getting butter'
—how right is the poet's fancy![25]
Truth is always rare and weakened
by one who from likes and dislikes is not free

In the transformation of society
Those people have been left wide-eyed,
The history of those have been neglected
Whose field of thinking has been limited

The mirror of contemporary times
Reflects only the present
Neither does history come alive again
Nor are its reflections infused with life

In the setting time of the Kulkar age
One step had been taken—
In the golden light of dawn
The confident second is ready to step ahead

In the lap of the Himalayas
Began the fall
of tiny little snowflakes
Naabhi, steadfast in his meditation,
Witnessed the birth of a new morn.

Notes

1. Existential truth refers to those which are found in nature and are in a sense the basis of life.
2. There are four gatis or states of existence according to Jain texts: naraki, tiryancha, manushya and deva: those living in hell, animals and birds, human beings and divine beings respectively.
3. The living being consumes and is consumed. It can be understood at the physical level literally, or as being consumed by passions, etc.
4. This is a continuation of the thought that no matter is either created or destroyed. They only change forms. So the same thing is called by a different name in a different context.
5. Jain philosophy believes there are collections of molecules called the skandas—these skandas are responsible for the functioning of the world. There are five such skandas.
6. Avasarpini is the phase of time when destructive forces are dominant.
7. Utsarpini is the phase of time when constructive forces are dominant.
8. A division of time.
9. Mythologically, the Kalpavriksha was believed to be the wish-fulfilling tree which could grant a person any object that he wished for.
10. Triphala is an Ayurvedic remedy literally meaning 'three fruits'. The three fruits are haritaki, amalaki and bibhitaki. It's the synergy of these three healing elements which gives triphala its curative powers for cleansing the system.
11. There are said to be ten types of Kalpavrikshas. The three verses give the names and products obtained from the ten types.
12. Vajrarishabhanarach is a bone joint in which three bones are held together by making a hole through all three of them and are joined on both sides by bones. This is called vajra. This is the strongest bone structure. The three types of bones which are held together are narach, ardhanarach and rishabhanarach (from *Jain Tattva Vidya* by Acharya Mahapragya).
13. Heaven is used for here for the word nirjarlok.
14. Chittasamadhi could be interpreted as finding bliss/peace in inner repose, repose in the soul. There are ten types of chittasamadhi mentioned in the Jain texts, primarily for ascetics. They are measures of rectitude in character through which one can find peace and restfulness and live in harmony with the soul.
15. Kalpataru is another name for the Kalpavriksha.
16. Kalpavriskha, Kalpataru are all names of the wish-fulfilling tree.
17. Anekanta is the principle of relativity or non-absolutism, which says truth is multi-dimensional; it helps us understand relativity. So nothing is totally

independent, everything is interrelated. This also means opposites coexist and so is a very inclusive philosophy.

18. Four states of existence as mentioned above: naraki, tiryancha, manushya and deva.
19. There were seven Kulkars or chieftains.
20. Kul means family lineage or clan.
21. Acharya Mahapragya says that we do not know about the embryo before it comes into the womb and we do not know the journey that it undertakes after death. In this context the paragraph has been interpreted.
22. Chandrayasha was the wife of Chakshushman.
23. This phrase means seasons change. Both peas and millet cannot be grown together. They belong to different seasons.
24. Anekanta is the principle of relativity as explained earlier. It goes to the credit of Acharya Mahapragya that he highlighted the relevance of this philosophical idea to every day life. According to anekanta, opposites coexist, truth is relative and the complete truth is never completely known.
25. Indra too has difficulty getting butter is a commonly used aphorism to say even the gods have a problem getting the best.

Canto II

The next canto begins where we left Naabhi, the last Kulkar, whom we saw engrossed in deep meditation. In his meditation he saw transformation. While he was still watching the future, his wife Marudev came running to him saying she had had a dream, a dream which she thought portended well.

She had dreamt of fourteen different things. The first was a wide-chested bull which seemed to be entering her mouth. Then she dreamt of a giant elephant having four tusks; a lion; Goddess Lakshmi seated on a lotus; a garland of flowers; the full moon; the sun; a fluttering flag; a purnakalash, a pond full of lotus flowers; a sea of milk; a celestial vehicle; a heap of gems and smokeless fire. Seven verses describe these fourteen items.

Purnakalash is an interesting concept full of imagery and so the word has been retained as it is. The kalash or pot is a metal one with a large base and a small mouth and when it has a coconut balancing on it, it is called purnakalash or the pot which is full. It is considered auspicious. Often, two eyes are depicted around the kalash symbolizing right faith and right knowledge.

Naabhi was excited with his wife's dream and prophesied that a very bright star was coming into their lives. And then a pair of radiant twins were born. The boy was named Rishabha because of the magnificent white bull which entered Marudev in her dream. The birth of the twins gave great joy to the parents and so the girl was called Sumangala.

The story goes on that somewhere else another pair was born. On that fateful day, this pair of children went to play while the parents sat a little distance away and watched. While the two of them were playing beneath a palmyra tree, a fruit fell on the boy's head leading to instant death. This was the first death due to accident in the world. It was also for the first time that one of the twins was bereaved.

No one knew how to look after a single person who was without her partner. While looking for a solution and ways to assuage their bewilderment, the people requested Rishabha to marry this lonely girl Sunanda too. It would give her support, they said. The marriage was performed.

And Acharya Mahapragya says this also set the example for polygamy in society.

The incarnation of Rishabha

Unmoving ground, unmoving sky
In the still air there were vibrations
In the repository of nature's poetry
Broke open a chorus in recitation

Quiet the moments of the night, quiet the state of mind
All the directions paused in silence
Half-asleep, half-awake
A dream world began to take shape

Beneath the wish-fulfilling tree
The age was in deep, happy slumber
In the night setting in from the west
Marudev's inner being came eloquent[1]

The vision came of a broad-chested bull
Ready to do the duties delineated[2]
Atop the eastern snow mountains high
Like an elephant he in dignity stands[3]

The strong, conquering and courageous
descends from the heavens[4]
Lotus-seated Lakshmi's presence
the attraction becomes[5]

The garland knit with spring flowers
Has come to decorate and ornament[6]
With its glistening white rays the moon
Enchants the night with her light[7]

Spreading the net of desire, the sun
destroys the darkness of the intense night[8]
In the fluttering wings of the flag
the imminent future is prophesied[9]

Fragrant flowers nectar-filled, cool water ponds
This purnakalash[10] is full anew
In the lotus pond, around the lotus
the bees are humming abuzz[11]

The milky waves of the kshirsagar[12]
Are enjoying their silent dance
A celestial vehicle in the sky
Is brilliant with the aura of the heavenly beings[13]

Equal to a collection of stars, bright as day
Glistening are the heaps of gems[14]
The blessings of the smokeless fire
Spread to all the ten directions[15]

Illumined directions held by delighted elephants[16]
Gained life and sprung up
Seeing Marudev ebullient, Naabhiraj[17]
opened his eyes wide and looked up

Naabhi

Tell me why you have come this second
With joy oozing out of your every cell
Has the wish-fulfilling tree sprouted
In this new courtyard of life?

Marudev

Said Marudev, yes, yes, yes
I have seen the greatest wonder
Lord, in the mirror of my mind
The lines of what I saw are etched

I don't know why today, suddenly,
a wave of joy has come gushing forth
Silent ocean, kissing the skies,
rises in a resounding cheer

Experience, alas, has no word power
Speech is always bereft of experience
How do I word my emotions?
Such moments are very rare!

Naabhi

Looks like something new will happen
That which has never occurred before
Holding the sacred lamp of hope
Runs every drop of blood through the being

Engrossed, still in meditation,
The consciousness has become thoughtless
Blessed it is by gaining touch
of the light of internal realization

Auspicious, propitious, auspicious, propitious
That which is to happen bodes well
A child, greatest of the great, is to be born
To sow the seeds of creation

The first rays of the sun
Touched the feet of Naabhi and Marudev
And declared the prophecy fine
Of a brilliant, auspicious time ahead

Birth of the twins

Nourished by natural food
A lifestyle synchronic with nature
A simple mind making way for natural birth
And all activity nature-sustaining

The birth of twins gave a glimpse
of the transformation of the times to come
To the bird imprisoned in the cage
It gave the sky to fly across

Children are born every day
But today something new has taken place
With the coming together of all directions
In the courtyard of life, a jewel has been embedded

The fragrant breeze is serenading music
To the accompaniment of pipes
The flame of the forest turned brilliant saffron
And the flowers stretched languorously

Naabhi and Marudev's hearts
Were full of joy
In this lineage of Kulkars
Had come this blessed birth

Naming the child

At the time of naming
Marudev's only point was that she had dreamt
of a powerful one who held the emblem of a bull[18]
The name of Rishabha was thus unopposed

Congrats! Congrats! They said in unison
All the pairs were delighted
Getting the name of Rishabha
He delighted even the flowers

The girl was called Sumangala
Auspicious, brilliant time it was
In chieftain Naabhi's house today
A great celebration made the day

Childhood

Under the clear and beautiful, expansive sky
On the earth which gave soft support
Blessed to rest on father Naabhi's lap
While the sun gave the firmness of resolve

The body, the tool to carry on life,
Is attained with good fortune
So pure and beautiful was its reflection
that the gross and subtle merged, transparently[19]

Wondrous beauty, golden-hued skin
With not a trace of flaw
His breath was fragrant as the lotus
Not a blemish on his person left

Aroused was desire equal amongst all couples
To see this child of wondrous beauty
To see this child who radiated
The gift of extra-sensory perception he was born with

Learning to walk in a short time
His speech was sweet to hear
With charming smiles, the young ones
aroused everyone's desire to embrace them

The simple act of thumb sucking
Gave him nutrition sweet as honey
Fruit diet improved his health
When the foundation is healthy, the body is too

It is not only on this earth
that living beings exist
From places like Uttarakuru[20] too
came fruits for nourishment

A bright child steals the heart
The dull wallows in its own tedium
If maturity does not colour the outlook
Life becomes a meaningless book

Taking boys of the same age
Games were taught to them
Dust on the golden bodies
Endeared them to their parents too

When physical training was being given
One child held Rishabha's finger in disregard
Drawing a breath deep he exhaled
The force of it sent the child far away

Childlike he was only in body
In thinking mature he was
The life of a great man is exemplary
A wonder of magnitude

Youth

Having conquered the first part of the day
The sun came up after noon
In an instant, buds gained
The status of full blooms

In every part of the great one
Youth was poised pretty
Expressed is the tree, unexpressed the seed
Life is but its shade

In the Age of Twins, youth has many long years
Those of childhood are but few
In the time of Snigdhakal[21]
Lies the capacity to quickly grow to one's potential

Health and work efficiency
Bring brightness to the pairing couples
Progressive and improved intellect
Sprouting like fresh saplings bright

A body without wrinkles, black hair
May the blue lotus-like eyes be filled with joy
Embodying enthusiasm, expressive of keenness
Are the ornaments of youth no doubt

Influence of the Avasarpini Age:[22] untimely death

As the Avasarpini Age progressed
The pace of life's chariot changed
Quiet times were destroyed
Even the Ganga turned her course

Sitting beneath the palmyra tree were
the twins with their new twin babies
Their eyes, which alone could have told the future,
Were covered by their own hands

Who has been able to recognize the
order of events in the world invisible to the eye?
We do not know among the fruits untouched
Which is ripe and which is not

In play both the children
Came beneath another palmyra tree
Innocent hearts, they could not
Read the script of transformation there

The arrow of the times moved easily
One fruit from the tree fell down
as a thunderbolt on the little boy's head
Complete silence too fell along with it

Cruel fate made the soft head
Lifeless in just a stroke
Vulnerable as the little girl child was, too early
the light in her life was snuffed out[23]

First time to see death
It was not easy to understand
Unheard of and unseen events
are difficult for the heart to cope with

She could not move, could not speak
Mental space became a void
Like a statue she stood motionless
Life, alas, had slipped away

Sitting far away the mother and father[24]
Felt their bodies go suddenly limp
The unassuaged trembling of the mind
Was as though life had stopped in its tracks

They came to the compound of the palmyra tree
And saw what they never had seen
Spoke the eyes, but in their hearts
Were drawn the lines of doubt

One is sleeping, one is standing
One motionless, one alive
Of the same age they were both
Now different in body and consciousness

First time for a father
That he was separated from his child
Even the restless mind was arrested
Into contemplation of grief

The age could handle death in course of time
Untimely ones they had never known, so
the question could not be contained
And the state of mind became weakened thus

Come, Sunanda! Said the couple
Asked she, 'How to go forward?'
Brother, in this state of sleep,
I will never be able to meet again

Then the mystery of death was elucidated
The inner self was torn apart
The fabric of life, alas,
Was torn to shreds too soon

Sunanda

Father, where is my brother?
Why did he leave me and go?
One eager to bloom flower
Has even before his time, gone away

A wilted flower will not bloom
Father, is this the meaning of death?
What is this creation-destruction cycle
Has this always been the way of life?

Father

Waves rise and fall in the ocean
Now again they rise to fall again
This is the story of life and death
Like the once lit wick extinguished

Sorrow gives perspective
This flow of thought is not untrue
It is sorrow which has found the path to truth
And yet everyone loves only happiness

The funeral rites were unknown
Now their feet have moved forward
And breaking and mending have come along
In these bonds of relationships

Nourished by her parents
The young girl now grew into a young maiden
Days went past and the memory of the brother
dimmed away to make space for new thoughts

In the meanwhile Mahakal[25]
Had spread itself out
The unexpected end of the twin
Was like a shadow of the passing clouds

You are like a deer strayed away
from the herd, roaming alone
All the supports seem to have fallen by
And the eyes beheld a vacuum

Being two is to be fearless, brother
The meaning of fear is to be alone
Duality is true in the dualistic world
Ahead of the guru is the disciple

A directionless kind of state came to be
No path was determined clear
Pervading was indecision on one's duty
What to do and not to do were undefined yet

Twin dead, but Sunanda,
Neither dead nor alive
Without shelter is the soul
Life is one of dependence

All the couples saw this maiden
Bereft of shelter and support
And thus was born the tale of the
changes in the dark Age of Twins

She met some couples who asked in curiosity,
Who are you and from where do you come?
How come in this world of pairs
You bring the idea of the lone one?

Speech fell silent, forgetting its prowess
The vocal chords fell into disuse
Throat sore, tears continuous
Became the tool for self consolation

Reassured by couples
A little comforted she became
Told them her life story
And how rudderless she felt alone

Request of the couples

To Kulkar Naabhidev[26]
All the couples went
With compassion they poured out to him
The story of the past event

Death in childhood had created
doubts in the Age of Twins
See, my Lord, a maiden alone
is in a state of helplessness

There should be an irrefutable solution
From which there is no going back
We twins should remain couples, for only then
can there be fearlessness and a peaceful reign

Our Lord of propriety and good conduct,
May this maiden prosper in you refuge
Like the philosopher's stone which by touch
turns all into gold, so may this maiden be

By becoming Rishabha's exalted consort
A new opening can be found
A new picture can then be created
In hues of myriad colours

Naabhi

It is a good proposition, yours
It truly appeals to the mind
The need is for deep reflection
When desire tempts the mind

It is difficult times for food
Even clothing is hard to get
Thanks to the compassion of the Kalpavriksha
Everyone's mind is at rest

Very few homes have survived the famine
The story is of the travails of the pair
Not visible is the solution
This head is bowed in despair

Bursting forth in the world of pairs
Are sparks of conflict and in-fighting
Lethargic and limp-like
Is the sparkler of self-discipline

Tell me, in difficult times, how
to give a solution to this problem
Here is a lion roaming hither and thither
How to give his roar a tune?

Pairs

The name of the solution is Rishabha
Within him all will be subsumed
When an eternal light like Rishabha is born
Why will pitch darkness ever consume us?

Only that parent will worry
Who does not have Rishabha with him
O great one, read the course of the future
How brilliant the lines look on his palm

Naabhi

Blessings! Blessings! But one problem
Existence in twins has been our life
Rishabha's twin is Sumangala
Let us hear what she has to say

Sumangala

Father Naabhi, great joy will be mine
If good befalls this girl
That person will have to be helped across who in the
dense forest, has lost her feet in quicksand

Acceptance by Naabhi

The desire of all the couples,
Organized by the Kulkar chief, is same
With Rishabha's approval and support
Only the rituals seem to be left

The new order of two wives
Will be accepted as rule
Polygamy henceforth will
Root itself in society

Towards the new direction of this new age
We have moved a step forward
Accept do I in solemn respect
The change of order we have brought about

Successful have been the efforts of the pairs
Sunanda has been blessed today
Religious texts can matter only thus far
Human concerns greater are.

Notes

1. Referring to Marudev's dream. The seven verses following describe that.
2. This is the first thing she saw: a bull, and so her child was named Rishabha.
3. The second thing she saw in her dream was an elephant as majestic as the Himayalas.
4. She also saw a powerful lion, the king of the jungle.
5. She saw the auspicious Lakshmi seated on a lotus.
6. Marudev dreamt of a garland of flowers.
7. The dream continues as she sees the moon and then the sun.

8. The sun shines destroying all darkness.
9. The next among the fourteen things Marudev dreamt of was the flag.
10. Purnakalash is an interesting concept full of imagery and so the word has been retained as it is. It was another object in Marudev's dream. The kalash or pot is a metal one with a large base and a small mouth, and when it has a coconut balancing on it, it is called purnakalash or the pot which is full. It is considered auspicious. Often, two eyes are depicted on the kalash symbolizing right faith and right knowledge. Reference: *Jainism: A Pictorial Guide to the Religion of Non-violence* by Kurt Titze and Klaus Bruhn, Motilal Banarsidass, 1998.
11. Marudev also dreamt of a lotus pond.
12. Kshirsagar means the milky ocean and that appeared in Marudev's dream.
13. She saw a celestial vehicle full of heavenly beings.
14. She dreamt of gems.
15. Marudev dreamt of fire without smoke.
16. Cosmologically, it is believed that elephants hold up the world, standing in the four directions.
17. Naabhi, the last Kulkar, and Marudev's husband.
18. Rishabha means bull. Since Marudev had dreamt of a bull, she suggested her child be named Rishabha. This was acceptable to all. The symbol of Rishabha, today, is the bull. Every Tirthankara is associated with an animal symbol.
19. Gross and subtle are the words used to indicate the sthool and sookshma particles, that is, the ones that are visible to the eye are called gross, and that which are not visible to the eye are called subtle. In this case the gross, or what was visible to the eye, was so pure that one can see even the subtle--a poetic exaggeration of its purity.
20. Uttarakuru is sometimes understood as a mythical land. In Jain cosmography, Devakuru and Uttarakuru are the two places where humans live. Both of them are found on the island continent of Jambudvipa.
21. The time before Rishabha is referred to as Snigdhakal. Also, the first three phases of Avasarpini and the last three phases of Utsarpini are called Snigdhakal. In Snigdhakal, the land is fertile and high-yielding.
22. Time is cyclical. The rising or progressive part of the cycle is called Utsarpini, and the regressive or descending part of the cycle is called Avasarpini.
23. The boy was the light in her life because their lives were so closely intertwined. It was not known what one twin would do without the other.
24. The story goes that a couple were sitting at a distance from where their children were playing. Their children were playing under a tree when the accident happened.
25. Mahakal refers to Yama or death.
26. Rishabha's father.

CANTO III

So Sunanda and Rishabha got married. There was no sacred altar, no specific mantras, no rituals. The mind tied the knot of belonging. Soon both Sunanda and Sumangala gave birth to children. Sunanda gave birth to one pair of twins. Sumangala gave birth to fifty pairs of twins. There has been a lot of debate on who is whose son; Acharya Mahapragya says in *Rishabha and Mahavira* (a collection of discourses he gave on the first few cantos of *Rishabhayan*) that a sutra in the Samavayang says Sumangala was Bharata's mother, which means Sunanda was Bahubali's mother. There were ninety-nine sons and two daughters. The daughters were Brahmi and Sundari, Brahmi beng Bharata's twin and Sundari, Bahubali's.

As Rishabha's family grew, so did their spiritual stature. Rishabha was blessed with avadhi gyana.

According to Jainism, there are five types of gyana or knowledge. The first is mati gyana or the knowledge gained through the senses, experience and thought. The second is sruti gyana or knowledge that is passed on through words and reason. The third is clairvoyant knowledge, which is known as avadhi gyana; the fourth, mahaparyaya gyana or telepathy; and finally, keval gyana, which is absolute knowledge that brings infinite awareness of all substances.

Through avadhi gyana Rishabha could comprehend why people were coming to him and what solutions were needed.

Amongst the people, the curiosity that the first marriage had inspired gave way to frustration brought about by the paucity of resources and the ensuing struggle for survival. The produce from the wish-fulfilling tree was becoming insufficient to meet everyone's needs. The number of mouths to feed was increasing. If, says Acharya Mahapragya, people could have learnt to share and eat, the situation would not have gone out of hand. But human nature is inclined to greed and avarice and the fight for the lion's share of the available resources left the people with no alternative but to seek governance. And so the idea of governance was born. It had a simple and specific purpose: to ensure equitable distribution of resources.

The people went to Rishabha and asked him to become the king and rule over them. Rishabha suggested they approach Naabhi for instructions. Naabhi anointed Rishabha as the king. Acharya Mahapragya relates how Rishabha defined the idea of the king: a king is everyone's master; he has a kingdom with a capital; he has an army; he has the power to punish, and ministers who will look after the matters of the state. The king is one who will prevent the exploitation of the weak and the dominance of the strong and also help in the development of good qualities.

The new king had many problems before him. He had to organize the people not just in terms of their food, but, realized Rishabha, that if a kingdom was to be set up the people would need to be organized at every level. Every action would have to be sustainable. Where would they live? How would they find food in the absence of yield from the Kalpavriksha?

As the king, weighed down by the responsibility of his position, sat with his brows knit in worry, the king of Devaloka, Saudharma, appeared before him and told him not to worry. He would build cities and dwellings. So it was that the housing problem was solved.

Rishabha taught them agriculture. He taught them to eat the harvested grain. But raw grain could not be digested. So he taught them to cook. They learnt that the hard way. They threw all the grain into the blazing forest fire. Since times had changed, the Dushma period brought dryness into the Sushma period which had been humid. The dryness caused a forest fire to take place. The fire had a lovely hue and the people tried to touch it and burnt their hands. They threw the grain into the fire to cook it but found the fire swallowed it all!

So pottery came to be.

The story of a civilization was now building up.

Organization of the kingdom

Flowing poetry unfettered by meter is bliss
Morning adorned by a thousand sunrays is beautiful
The lotus of life is blooming and radiant every day
Such pleasures are inexpressible by the tongue

Bliss in Naabhi's family, contentment in his home and hearth
Reciprocal response from within and without
The duality of the inner and outer still unknown
Their oneness makes the warp and weft of simplicity

The wedding drew close at the auspicious hour
The first presence of the family as an entity
In twins had been defined a dual state of existence
Came the new definition of a plural group as family

Wonder, curiosity, enthusiasm in each one present
Lightning-like queries probed the mind
How will this unknown institution command respect?
To be sure, the home will a battlefield become

This is universal law: whenever a new situation presents itself
The shadow of doubt clouds the sky
Like the early winter mornings which are foggy
But still allows the sunlight to pierce through

Having obtained approval from Naabhi
Blessed spring danced in the garden of life
The first instance of polygamy
The first wave of relationships legal

No construction of a wedding area
Nor a yagya mandap[1] by name
No fire as the ceremonial witness
Everything now unknown

No pundit to recite the mantras
No mantras to recite
Paanigrahan[2] alone
Defined the act of marriage

A new chapter had now been written
On social conduct and living
At the end of every age
A new order has always come to be

The union of minds alone
Defines true marriage
A social event it is now becoming
Life itself led by the trend

Come, let us move on, something new will happen today
The husband of these two maidens will be one man
Each of the many twins present is full of disbelief
Such a surprising event in the Age of Twins!

Gathered the community of twins, strong their curiosity
Well endowed is man's intellect and yet for more he is thirsty
Sri Naabhi and Rishabha brought together their family
And the wind blew into the reeds to make music

In their eager eyes flashed their joy
Sri Naabhi's blessings for this maiden came from deep within
May she be by Rishabha accepted
May a new respect for women surge anew

Indeed! Indeed! Indeed! This was necessary, necessary
To this moment of change witness, we are witness
May this arid land be irrigated to be made fertile
May the life of these people of the desolate land be joyous

Sacred consummation of giving one hand into the other
Pleasant as the pitter-patter of raindrops
Establishment of a new age and order by Rishabha
Indeed many dimensions has this life eternal

Pristine surroundings and a blemish-less mind
Few were the requirements of life
Life was pleasant and of long duration
But Rishabha himself a bodiless state experienced

Dreams have association with man since aeons
The subconscious mind in sleep is awakened
Delighted and excited came Sumangala when
Rishabha was experiencing the stirrings of awakening

Said she that a garland of dreams she had seen
On the divine night when a cup of nectar did she drink
Bright future is yours lady! 'Your son,' he said,
'Emperor will become, the shining star of the Kulkar age.'

At the auspicious hour came the birth of the twins
All nature was with joy exuberant
The dictionary two new words gained
Grandfather-grandson—a new relationship was found

The son named Bharata was the harbinger of a bright future
The daughter named Brahmi brought a new dawn
Pure Sunanda became the mother of twins
Born was Bahubali, brother to Sundari, and strong in form

The wheel of time turned and offspring in number grew
Sumangala had the highest of blessings received
Ah! She became mother of fifty pairs as her brood grew
And so swayed the tree of joy in Rishabha's porch

Beginning of governance

Impatient with the circumstances, annoyed in the mind
The twins came to meet Sri Rishabha in solitude
And said, 'We support you alone, our Lord!
O omniscient one, look, here is a problem of magnitude

In this rare flow of time into the period of Sushma
The three punitive measures have reached their peak
The fire of anger, the chaos of greed,
And abusive words have all taken steps forward

The Kalpavriksha too is peeved
The hungry are seeing stars even during day
In search of alternative sources on which to feed
We have come to you to seek solutions today.'

The cry of pain is more piercing than arrows, when
the farmer ploughs a field sown with sorrow
The innermost desire of the twins was
easily understood because of empathy

Rishabha's inner mind full of compassion
And his sense of responsibility too came on its own
Memory of his past lives, developed intuition
Living in consciousness in his last birth

In these times of conflict, a king is essential
He will start a new order
This time period is one of great changes
Abide one should by the discipline of the ruler

Become king and ease away everyone's sorrow
O destroyer of problems, rid us of all our distress!
You alone have the right to rule
Who else here can measure up to you?

Go! Go seek the shelter of Naabhi's presence
With his every step a king he will give you
Give us a king, we have come as petitioners
And seek answers from none other than you

So it will be, so it will be, Rishabha your king will be
Give up mourning, having drunk of the pure flow of this news
Excited, inspired, the twins came running
With difficulty did they keep their feet on the ground

Lord, today a new sunrise on the horizon there will be
With these hands we will the new king anoint
Brought we have the holy waters of all the rivers
None of these things are to you unknown

Content and unbiased was Rishabha's body language
His ten fingers in the mudra[3] of relaxation, cupping his palms
he poured holy water to consecrate the beautiful moment
While the glowing aura of honesty added the final touch

Restlessness got the blessing of assurance
Assurance which became synonymous with the position of the king
Everyone loves his independence
But hunger destroys this love

If the Kalpavriksha had not revealed their miserliness
If man could have learnt to share and eat
Then a reign imbued with the power of the ruler
would never have sat on man's head

Similarity in man's memory and intellect
Dissimilarity in his aggression, conduct and thinking
This imbalance is the one that gives the invitation
To weapons and acts punitive

Kingdom and its rule

The one who worries about everybody is the king
Dedicated to this larger duty is his life
The first step is to ensure food
For the betterment of their physical well-being

These events that cause disorder will cease only
when the state ensures the hungry have food in their belly
Engrossed in meditation he saw in the depth of depths
A lightning flash naturally tearing apart the sky

Fruits, leaves, roots will be the edibles
Cultivated easily, the stomach also they will fill
This secret of nutrition some twins understood
And took Rishabha's message far and wide

How to solve the housing problem?
How to spread an expansive tent across the sky?
The Lord could not research and innovation command
At this time descended a celestial being[4]

Islands and water bodies there are many
Countless galaxies there are in the sky
In this unique world we are not alone
On every land mass there is celebration[5]

The king of a beautiful world (Devaloka) I am, O Lord!
Desirous of being of service to you
Man's relationship with earth age-old
There is always the story of coming and going

Worry is writ large on the king's knitted brows
Worry could be seen swaying his thoughts
In a trice I will the housing problem solve
In creating a town I will be successful

Help is mutual between all human beings
Its understanding reflected in every uttered word
Just for your signal we await, O leader of men!
For initiation into the beginnings of human civilization

O Lord, divine presence man has gained
The skies sing the praise of this virtual world
O Lord, divine power has come forth
At crossroads now, this age has found its desired goal

Blessed we are, gaining direction, content is our mind
There is great interest in the people to explore new ideas
Indra called Kubera forthwith and the
art and secret of town planning was imparted

Divine energy is immeasurable, unimaginable
Constructed was artistic, unique and beautiful,
Palaces, houses, barracks as desired
The twins now began living under a roof

Having finished his work, satisfied he came
to the feet of the Lord and bowed
Lord, sanctify the palace we have built
By taking the first step on this hitherto unknown path

Entry of the forest-dwellers into a town
As though the ocean is being filled into a pot
The twins came to know it as their home
The ground beneath the roof and the sky above

Food and shelter the twins had got
Full of possibilities is the world of illusions
Indigestion of the uncooked grain was the first disease
How to eat? Guide us, O compassionate one!

Crush, grind and eat the healthy grain
Enjoy and enthuse the digestive system
His order they followed and yet the problem persisted
Transformation demands unswerving patience

Fashion a cup with leaves, dip it in water
With the warmth of your palms rub it so it's edible
The wet fruit will become soft and digestible
Will be nutritious and sweet

Food was tasty and taken in very small quantities
Grain is difficult to digest and so seemed large in portion
Soaked and sun-dried grains were also consumed
But the problem of indigestion remained

The memory of the Kalpavriksha was recalled
Food had never been such a source of worry
An accidental event took place in the forest
Every branch was aglow as though with lightning

In a troubled mind, thoughts and activity levels are high
But nature, in the mouth of an oyster, pearl becomes
A sudden event took place in the forest
From every tree a brilliant light burst forth

The twins saw this as an offering of brilliance
So far unknown, this is a glimpse of the future
Eagerly to touch they extended their hands
In the heat of the fire they got burnt, they got scorched

They came running to Lord Rishabha
Lord, what has come to be, we do not understand
Its alluring and so one desires to touch it
But being heartless it burns the one who touches

Self-realized Rishabha saw through meditation
The fire element was raising the levels of mercury
When moisture alone or dryness alone exists
Then nowhere and at no time can fire be born

Two ages of dryness and moisture[6] have come together
Yes, fire has manifested itself
Said Lord Rishabha, cook your grains in this
Then eat after chewing well

Treasuring his directions, they went back to the forest
The Lord's order is the most revered aspect of life
Bringing the grains, they threw them into the fire
In a storm, when has a cup got filled with water?

All the grains vanished in the fire and running back they came
Offering the flower of their dedication at his feet, they said
The hungry fire eats up everything
The one who goes within returns not

Ignorance alas! Ignorance all the sorrows gives
Nourishes the seed of sorrow unstinted
Now understand first the way to take life forward
And recognize your duty as is wont.

Notes

1. Yagya mandap is the area where a fire is set up at the centre and sacred ceremonies are conducted around it with the fire as witness.
2. Paanigrahan literally means giving the hand of the bride into that of the groom. In one meeting, Acharyaji had told me that this is the most beautiful and important act of marriage. Trust is thus reposed. Therefore the original word has been retained.
3. Mudras are symbolic body postures and hand gestures.
4. The king of Devaloka is called Saudharma.
5. The poet is imagining the stars to be a mark of festivity (as lights or lamps) and so is saying that there is celebration elsewhere too.
6. The period of dryness is associated with the Dushma period while that of moisture with the Sushma period. This was the time when the age was being transformed from Sushma to Sushma-Dushma.

CANTO IV

An empathetic king began his rule.

The occurrence of fire opened the doors to progress. The art of fashioning vessels, weapons, clothes, pictures and sculptures came into being. Vessels were needed for cooking. Weapons and instruments were required for construction and agriculture, and so metallurgy was born. Social life necessitated the construction of houses and weaving. The profession of barbers came into being for personal groming: to cut the hair and nails. Agricultural labours, traders and defence personnel also came into existence after the people learnt the use of fire.

Simultaneously learning and education were also developing. Rishabha is said to have taught his son Bharata seventy-two arts, and his son Bahubali the art of lakshan vidya or the knowledge of every kind of living being. To his elder daughter Brahmi he taught the eighteen scripts. To his younger daughter Sundari he taught mathematics. The use of bow and arrow, the nitty-gritties of economics and medicine, and even games he explained to the people. It is said that even though these tasks did not fall in the sacred or the divine category, and worse, they were activities that attracted the karmic particles, Rishabha involved himself in them so as to help human beings lead their life on earth. Here Acharya Mahapragya talks of the importance of doing one's duty whatever it may entail.

As knowledge and the number of material objects in society began to grow, attachment to them also began to sprout. Familial bonds came to be established based on such attachments. The idea of a 'rich' man and a 'successful' man began to take root. The idea of 'me' and 'mine' followed.

Society was organized into the following categories. Those who defended the nation were called Ugr. The ministers were called Bhoj. Advisors or regional chiefs were called Rajanyas and all the others were called Kshatriyas. Initially, the three punishments of the Kulkar age worked well, but soon, sterner reprimands were required and the punishment of mandalbandh or restricting the offender to a certain geographical space came to be implemented.

The race came to be known as the Iskhvaku race because Rishabha taught them to drink the juice of sugar cane. Sugar cane juice also plays a major role in the next canto when it is served as the only food that Rishabha can partake of as a monk. Sugar cane is also used to illustrate the excitement of consumption: while you are partaking of it, it may be sweet but once the juice is drawn out, all that remains is a dry stem.

The first few steps of society building

For social harmony, the need
is for a leader to be created
For the fertility of land, the need
is for rain-bringing clouds to pour

The feelings of sorrow and joy remain
the oldest features of human nature born
Destruction of sorrow and creation of joy
Have always been man's employ

The one who experiences the other's grief
As intensely as his own
To him comes the mighty honour
Of leading society to the fore

For the people of this land, today
Rishabha's guidance is a must
On him rests the charge of giving
to this new age, the right direction

Out of his dwelling limits went the Lord
Taking the pairs with him
Soon the fingers of the potter began
to dig the ground for clay

Kneading it with water himself
He gave it the shape to hold
Fired in a kiln, it became
the first vessel, lo and behold!

The craft of the potter
Became a tradition set
And a textual treatise was built around
the profession for its techniques

Put the grains into the pot
And place it on the fire
Eat cooked food easily
To indigestion wave goodbye

The first step in cooking was taken
And now visible the first boil
Sometimes in silence
Sometimes with incessant chatter[1]

The development of iconography and the concept of duty

With desire, desire deepens
Desire has its own cycle
Just as milk ferments to give curd
And curds in turn, to butter gives way

Necessity, necessity
Aloneness has no existence
With every relationship is built
The person of many bonds

After every new development comes
a lasting aftermath
The restlessness of the mind gives rise to
new and newer developments

For the sculptor to do his work
A metallurgist was required
For the metallurgist it was required
That a welder do his job

Order, disorder—both are at play
Some achievements come only with order
Yet others call for a major leap forward
Thereby creating a new order

Blessed is the age into which is born
The man with intuitive knowledge
Today the brilliant rays of Rishabha's knowledge
Have awakened the age's consciousness

The tradition of potters
Created the vessel to hold and eat food
The tradition of blacksmiths
Gave weapons, axes and tools

And the tradition of architects then
Resolved to build houses few
Agricultural land was clothed anew
as land to construct upon

The tradition of weavers
Gave clothes to cover oneself
The tradition of barbers
Gave haircuts and tonsured the head

From these five categories of tradesmen
The young society got its life
Like the blooming lotus that
draws its energy from the sun

With the plough the land was tilled
And in the virgin land seeds were sown
Seeing the growing crop the farmer wondered
And asked themselves, what marvel is this?

When harvested and thrown into the barn
The cattle began eating the grains
With a cloth cover the mouth was the order
This became the norm for all cattle then

So uninformed were they that
at every step they required instructions
They never did undo the mouth cover of the animals
Who could therefore never see freedom from it

The cows and bulls stopped eating
A new problem came to be
It is not easy to create, was the feeling,
A new man or a new age

Tie the mouth only when needed
Then they will eat when uncovered
Most difficult of jobs also relent to skilful tact
Like extraction of oil and butter

Fertile earth, ready to yield
Even without manure, rich
Rain showers drenched everything
O, the clouds wished for the summer sun!

Harvested grains made available to all
A new vocation came to be
The farmer grew crops and his occupation alone
Gave growth to one and all

Next came the desire to hoard
And then to safeguard with defence personnel
Agriculture gave birth to learning and soon the script
was born, leading in turn to skills and tools and building a social form

With training in farming, writing, weaponry
Society became efficient
That which has never happened before
Now came to be

The mind awakened to many a thought
It was necessary to develop education
Following education comes
Success, wisdom, fulfilment beautiful

For the progress and development of society
The first step of the ladder is language
With the growth of language alone
Science becomes long lived

For literature to blossom
Word felicity, sweetness of meter,
Ornamentation—the three together
becomes the crowning glory of eloquence

Development of education

Bharata, read the etymology of words
So the door to verbal felicity opens
Let meter and rhyme be internalized
As sugar that melts into milk

Read, daughters! In this world of action
Education will earn you respect
Education is the new incarnation
Of the Kalpavriksha of ancient times

At the right time, usage of the right tool
Will make life successful
The seed sown in fertile land will
naturally grow to bring glory

In the word, small as a pot,
comes the resolve to fill the ocean
For the prolific flow of speech
The script alone is the answer

To his left sat Brahmi
Whom he instructed in script
And to his right, to Sundari
He gave instructions in mathematics

In the instruction of script and math
The woman got a lead
In her beautiful inner self
A fragrant flower bloomed

A woman has no right to education
This myth was fostered in time
Forgetting Rishabha's design
This falsity has grown

Even birds and animals have been educated,
Why this story of depriving women
Long dark years of ignorance
Her lot was to weep in silence

The condition is clear, only that person
has the right to education
Who is endowed with intellect
Whether a man or woman that may be

Bahubali was given the knowledge
Of man, animals and even precious gems
At the threshold of dignity from knowledge
A light was lit to illuminate

The hidden energy in a small seed
Becomes a tree of a hundred branches
Seeking permission from the ocean
Even the pond becomes a source of water

Friends and relatives,
Spread the word of learning far
The sons of Manu[2] on earth
Laid the foundation for their life to build

Togetherness and the institution of family

My mother, my father, my sibling
My wife, my children
My house, my wealth
And so was strengthened the mantra of 'mine'

The idea of 'mine' gave shape
to the idea of family
Mine-ness alone is family
Such social boundaries were drawn

And so they moved a step towards marriage
And families began to multiply
In the social set-up marriage gained
a unique place as the basic social unit

With knowledge educated, with morality
imbued, capable became the people
The one without them was like an animal
Education alone is the heaven on earth

Moved by empathy for fellow beings
The mind grew holy and compassionate
Understanding the role of a leader
Rishabha taught the lesson of the times

One's own house, one's farmlands
One's forest, one's gardens
Decided with propriety—all people
Like the sword its scabbard got

When the rule of the atma prevails
Punishment is of no avail
It teaches the meaning of the rod
In more subtle ways to one and all

Harvest of the fertile fields
Sugar cane crops delight
From the cowshed comes the sound
of mooing cows from dawn to dusk

The use and basis of everything
was received from Lord Rishabha
On earth this was indeed
the very first phase of social life

Great was the shock when the Kalpavriksha
was no longer able to support
A feeling of being let down is inherent
in dependence; the self alone is reliable

What now? The families
of the Kulkars asked in fear
More frightening than hunger and thirst
Is, alas, the fear of hunger itself

Then the words of comfort came
Fear not, for to fear is to die
The essence of this life is to toil
Measure the worth of your hands

This precious oracle blew in
the mantra of fearlessness and effort
In the interplay of human skill and insentient matter
were established ways of livelihood

With the green fruit of such labour
The earth was adorned
Disappeared the fear of hunger
Replaced by a smile on every lip

Organization of the kingdom

Ugra was the name of the defence personnel
The powerful ones in defence
Accumulation, aggression, disagreements—all
became the characteristics of society

Partners in organizing state affairs
The ministers were called Bhoj
Through the ministers and their meetings
Were formed the rules of governance

Advisors or regional chiefs
Were known as Rajanyas
So decentralized became governance
Like the clouds dividing the sky

All the rest were called Kshatriyas
So people's vocations were ordained
When there is lack of organization,
Comes a plethora of perversions

Creator, giver and protector,
His words were paramount
The one a lasting solution gives
Becomes the leader beloved

The one who is not ready for service
But only carries the weight of his position
What king is he? What leader?
The whole world is troubled by him

Having gained power from the people
Does no good deed in turn
Grave remiss this
And deserving of condemnation

A small kingdom, accessible frontiers
And compassion in the leader's heart, so that
the ocean is no different from me
Thus thinks every drop

Having established, for the first time,
A happy relationship between the king and his subjects
Diverse thoughts and diverse tastes
Bound together in one tale

Long life, longevity
The population grew by leaps and bounds
Hard work, efficiency and with cooperation
Prosperity spread on all four sides

Self-discipline before disciplining others
Was the fundamental mantra of governance
Rishabha was under control
Because of his own self-discipline

Man, a puppet of circumstances
And by his very existence alone.
That which changes with the situation
Is not the original, but only its translation.

Karma operates on the human being through
fruition, accepted are the conditions of karma
As you do, so you reap
As the juice, so the taste

Time and nature, fate and intellect
Karma, circumstances—everything relative
This is the teaching of anekanta[3]
Only the source is absolute, all else relative

The pairs were bound by karma
And their mutual infatuation was controlled
When attachments are less and lifestyle Spartan
Controlled and calm is the ripening of karma[4]

But now times were moving on
Well-oiled, said the raconteur of society
Moments of anger, greed and passion
Seem well rehearsed when they manifest

Destruction of property comes
from too much self-obsession
Circumstances are but the stimuli from which
an embryonic fight turns into a rebellion

The beginnings of passions should
In childhood be quelled so that
they do not increase
and revolt against the present

The whole idea of punishment
Depends on your sense of shame
Every age has its mental make-up
Punishment is the science of a modern mind

When the sense of shame was strong
'Paribhashit' was the punitive measure
'Sit down here' were the king's
accusing, anger-filled words

Nature's laws were in balance
When the sense of shame grew less
The punitive measure of 'mandalibandh'
Or house imprisonment was adopted

This punishment meant they could not
Go beyond the identified area
If the culprit was hidden from view and tied up
He was getting the third type of punishment

When the inner passions flamed
Punishment acquired a new form
Till now what was verbal became physical
And the use of the stick became common

With self-discipline, knowledge increases
Wealth increases then on its own
Intellectual growth alone will
only increase mental tension

Limited governance, few crimes
Few punishments, arms unused
This is the greatness of Rishabha's rule
There is nowhere any doubt

Establishment of the Ikshvaku race
Fertile lands, irrigated with sap—every grain of sand
with sweetness filled, the mind brimming with pleasant thoughts
Joy permeating the earth and sky

In pristine nature, sweetness is desired
Sugar cane fields at every step
In a self-disciplined people
The sugar cane stick is never used to strike

To collect the juice and drink it
Rishabha gave directions
On every one's lips was written Ikshavku
And naturally the lineage got its name

The other name was Kashyapa
Rishabha became famous as the first Kashyapa
With the patronage of great people
A lineage becomes rich and continuous

The dignity and qualities of the Adipurusha[5]
Lent pride to the society whole
On every head as though there was
Ornamented a crown of flowers.

Notes

1. The poet has used the word vachal to mean the pot is boiling with a sound that he likens to chatter.
2. Manu is a title accorded to the progenitor of mankind.
3. Anekanta is a principle which has been explained earlier. The following lines elaborate that saying that all the variations we see in this world are relative. Only the source is absolute.
4. The ripening of karma is a concept which means that in every birth one accumulates some karmas: some good, some bad. It takes its own time to give the rewards or punishments in subsequent births. That process is called ripening.
5. Rishabha is reffered to as the Adipurusha or the first man—not physically but as the one who taught the ways of the world to humanity.

Canto V

So it was that crafts and delicacies like sugar cane juice began to enliven the newly formed society. This canto describes the festival of spring as it was celebrated in those times. It describes the navarasas (or nine rasas) into which human emotions were broadly classified. In classical style it talks of separation in love and the gamut of emotions that play in between.

From the nine rasas that symbolize life as it is, Acharya Mahapragya leads in the typical manner of progression of all Jain works to the rasa that is not among the nine, but is that of detachment or veetaraga.

How does veetaraga come about when the mood is of raga? Acharya Mahapragya introduces it with a story. It is said that flowers have the capacity to bring alive the past because they have been in this world since aeons, and so hold history. Once, when Rishabha came into the garden and saw people playing with flowers, he felt he had seen the vision earlier and then remembered it had been in heaven at such and such a time. Then he began recollecting his past. He observed that flowers bloom and perish; similarly, the cycle of life is transitory and material riches futile.

This thought triggered a journey deep within the recesses of

Rishabha's mind. And then he thought: I have created a society, organized it, established a kingdom and governance but, if along with all these attributes of consumption, if the ability to give up or renounce is not built, then society will never experience completeness. Unless there is a balance between the material and the non-material, there will be no harmony. He realized that in a society which is built with focus only on the material, there will always be imbalance, like that between the rich and the poor.

Therefore, he took the decision to renounce his kingdom. His family and the people of his kingdom were shocked to hear it. They found nothing wrong with consumption and they saw no point in renunciation. But Rishabha was firm, and dividing his kingdom among his sons, he left. But not before he had given them broad outlines on how a king should view his responsibility. He emphasized that a king had to be selfless, he must learn to conquer his desires. Most importantly, he told them to remember that the underlying principle of governance was the equality of all living beings.

Spring festival

A crowd of people in the forest
In the sky, the sun was alone
The bees driven by intoxicating fragrance,
Created is the ambience of the festival of spring

In every corner of the perfumed garden
Delighted are the flowers in bloom
Desire with youthful countenance peeps
Detachment, coyly closing its eyes

Comes spring in step with groom Chaitra[1]
Every pore in exuberance

In the pandal of creeper malati[2]
Humming bees set the tone
The sweet call of the cuckoo bird
Makes a melodious offering anon
Gently fanning, the wind blows past
On every lip a smile is borne

With sparkle like that of a firefly
Is the moist leaf of the sapling fresh
Echoing with the grasshopper's song
The night has spent itself out
The past becomes history, my friend,
Only the present inspires faith

Selecting the right flowers are the maidens
In postures as though engaged in yogasan
With the footsteps of the young men,
Every corner of the garden resounds
The sunlit sky without a cloud
And yet the earth below cool and calm

Adorning, captivating ornaments
Are the flowers everywhere
A festival it is for celebrating
Elegance, fragrance and beauty fair
Fertile nature in growing loveliness
The giver is truly never in want

The long branches of the tree bring
joy to the one who swings

Like the large black bee that
the rare flower with sweet nectar found
Laden with fruits feel the trees, as on every branch
a woman swings and young men laugh in tease

Adorned by a robe of flowers, the day
is opening up to the sun
Decorated with gardens
The month of Chaitra is vivacious
Seeing the world so dance with life,
the inner voice acquired expression

In the flowing river of joy, all people
are neck deep in blissful stupor
For among the navarasas,[3] sringar is indeed first
Just as sand sticks to the bare feet,
the leaves dance in grace with the wind
And laughter resounds in every budding flower

Gently blowing fragrant winds
are caressing every branch
As the wind moves ahead on its way
The tree feels the pangs of separation
Every cell is brimming with tears
Every branch trembling with the sorrow of parting

Enraged by the kicks from
the lover and his love in their play
was the flame of the forest with its red floral array
The inner mind is angry, and
like an actor playing the role of wrath
Clad as he is, in an orange garb

The speed of the wind caused
a wave to rise
Efficient wind, but how can
the waters bear the taunt?
Each has its own strength
Deep within it is recognized that coveting is not right

Walking hither and thither all the time
And yet fearless the deer
Languorous but steady-paced and brilliant in form
Endowed with colours naturally beautiful
Touching the earth at every step
With joy in its proud eyes

Under the canopy of creepers
Darkness spells terror
Through the bushy and dense forest
Sunrays travel in fear
In the warm lap of the lover, love is ensconced
In envy, even the king is left desiring

Climbing the trunk the dodder plant
Is exploiting the tree
What kind of person is he who
exploits others to feed the self
Alas! What a despicable act
Even shame is ashamed

Seated is Shri Rishabha Maheshwar
And he saw all around him
The lovely game of flowers
Which bore the mark of history long

Wondrous is the kingdom of the mind
Only churning it yields butter[4]

Activated were thoughts about material comfort
Everything seems exciting before consumption
Once partaken is left completely dry
Like the sugar cane after its juice is extracted
Then through avadhi gyan[5]
He saw all the attributes of matter across space

Incomparable is the comfort of the celestial being
Human comfort but a speck
Like a rivulet to the ocean
Or a small container
Keeping the mind entertained with frivolities
Is but the way delusion works

Influenced by sensory impulses human consciousness
believes life is successful
if all desires of the senses are satisfied.
There are many a treatise on comfort and happiness
Some begin where others end
While truth itself is lost in stupor

Richness of life fully explored
Only peace not manifested
Without peace, man
will be distressed at every step
If there be violation right at the beginning,
How will the desired goals be ever realized?

As greed grows
So does demoniac anger

Ego, illusion
Fear, jealousy, their repercussions
At that time dharma is necessary
For it makes action cultured

With the tender thread of maternal love
Is made a happy society
It is only the excesses of maternal love
Which reign over the human mind
Too much of maternal love
Can make one blind

Only when we see truth ourselves
Do we have the right
To understand truth
Or else closed is the door
Every step in this world is suggestive with implicit
meaning, but truth is covered, concealed

Creative knowledge, the intuitive perceived
Elaborated was the path of restraint
All texts seem inadequate before a true renunciate
A life of restraint is like spring all through the year
The earth and skies resound, saying
in every moment of such a life lives a saint

Got the willing support
Of the celestial beings of Brahmaloka[6]
To begin the dharma chakra
Now is necessary all support
Only consumption is wrought with problems
With excesses increase all disease

Inner impulse and inspiration
Presents a new morn
Unknown is the path of restraint
Now make it known to all
The future will be bright and brilliant
A fiery offering to fire itself

Indeed, with the thinking changed so
It got an actionable form
The eldest son Bharata[7]
Supportive of his father
Explained the principle of restraint
Which will fuel the world from now on

Here, take your responsibility
Sit on the throne, said Rishabha to Bharata
I will go on the path of restraint
Engrossed in my soul
A new age will thus begin
The beacon of the human race

Hearing words unknown, unimagined,
wondrous for the very first time
Giving up the throne, renouncing home
Given up will be this family
Given up will be the love for the self
And life will be filled with equanimity

Eyes brimming, speech quivering
The throat parched
Silent was the son, dumbfounded
Every second aware and yet unaware
Asked he, what kind of alternative this is
Lord, change your decision

Service at thy lotus feet
Gives the greatest of pleasures
How can I equate the clouds with
the ocean, O my Lord?
They may well roam the skies
But still with respect only to the earth

To walk in your presence, O lord
Gives unstinted blissful joy
Without you, even riding an elephant
Seems doubtful of giving such joy
You alone are my source of joy
You alone are the illuminating light

Under the shelter of your lotus feet
That shade gives a blissful experience
Under the shade of the umbrella
That cannot be found
You, O lord, are the natural protector
Like the forest is made blessed only with the Kalpavriksha

When to the lap of the west goes the sun
There lies the root of the night of darkness
On the aged body what beauty will bring
The finest muslin cloth?
You alone are everyone's lifeline
You are the security even for the lost

Where there is Rishabha, it is beautiful
Be it town or forest
Without Rishabha, all the wealth
does not conquer my mind
Like the chatak's[8] wait is for the dawn
And the chakor's[9] love for the moon

Rishabha replied, Unwavering is my determination
to renounce the kingdom
Unmoving I am like the Himalayas, son
With just one and only goal
Forget, forget all the other ideas, remember
Silence is preferred greatly over idle talk

The passion of the people makes
the king indispensable
The seesaw of anger and greed
Makes the ruler a must
Here accept the burden of this kingdom
The strength of the masses, you will be.

Gospel, the speech of the Lord
Yet, not acceptable to the heart
Looks like the kingdom is full of chaff
The grain is going far away
Rain, rain now, O clouds!
May the inner being be blessed

The command is to govern the country
That I have to follow
Establish new kingdoms I will
But the true state is that in which
the first phase is consumption, and
the second phase will be to accept yog[10]

In the face of the order, I am king
As is desired by the Lord
Only that will yield sweet fruit
Which is sweet to the Lord

In the seen how much is left unseen
And yet only the seen is desired

Coronate him, Bharata, as the king
Having got the Lord's message
Officials got busy in making preparations
With mixed feelings in their minds
To bring a new king to a throne
that was so respected and held sacred by all

With waters from different oceans poured on him
The coronation of the king was carried out
From Rishabha's rule Bharata's rule it became
A transformation in wisdom brought about
The new king requested in humility,
O Lord, advise me on governance and polity

Like rising from the snow-clad mountains
Comes the flow of continual waters,
The king takes from the people, on loan,
The power to mete out punishments
If however comes arrogance of power,
His reign indeed becomes sullied

Difficult, difficult in this world
The business of power
Everyone should get justice always
And means to overcome problems

Universal rule in a society
Made of different kinds of people
Some weak, some strong
The community itself teaching along

Against the weak the strong ones
Cannot mete out injustice
Such success of governance lies
in preventing possible exploitations

That will become easily possible
If the king is not greedy for wealth
Only he can do justice to the throne
Who is himself content

Unsuccessful is the king who has not conquered his desires
Like zero without a number preceding it
Gaining a balanced ruler
The earth is indeed blessed

The ruling principle of a cruel king
Is like a son bereft of love for his mother
Who, along with ruling, is sensitive
He becomes the harbinger of peace

People gain confidence in a kingdom
That has no thorns but only fragrance
Where every breath brings faith
There a peaceful sky extends

With only punitive measures
People's resentments rise
With only rewards and awards
People lose their bearings

Full with rewards and punishments
Administration will be free of problems
Using both measures to an optimum
Will be the true guardian of humankind

With one wheel alone
No chariot can move
The officials should give momentum to
The administrative chariot

The minister who knows governance
Brings prosperity to the masses
Then the kingdom gets the auspicious Sriyantra[11]
Which keeps it safe and forever free

A minister greedy for wealth
Wreaks havoc at every step
The ruler becomes the exploiter
Waste it is these fields to irrigate

Conflicts in the people's minds be gone
Should be the government's goal
If problems were to increase more
It's like feeding polluted water to all

They should not have the liberty
To use the common man as scapegoat
They should not have the liberty to become
A parasite and spread

To go along with every step
The mind should be filled with empathy
Melting with the pain of the people
Every cell should strain with effort

The essence of governance
Was thus advised to Bharata
To rule over the self by the self

And to look within
Delighted was everyone's mind
Every bit enjoying the lesson

Bahubali[12] got the kingdom of Bahali
Everyone was happy
In every street, in every corner
A new enthusiasm arose
In the equanimity of love like a mother's
The empire saw a brilliant new phase

The form and message of King Rishabha's kingdom

Not tormented by hunger anyone
No one assailed by poverty
Shelter for everyone comfortable
Nowhere is there an exception
There is no sorrow filling the heart
Balanced, vibrant flows the blood

No distinction between high born and low
All men are equal and alike
Distinction only on the basis of work
Everyone gets the same respect
As much beauty as there is in the sun
So much worth is also there in the moon

The dignity of Rishabha's great reign
Has to be preserved
The newly trodden path and those that were left behind
Have to be honoured too

The sutra for change is building anew
The sutra for stability is preservation

The music of the inner mind
Played on the strings of the heart
Bringing to life a new resonance
Vibrant, and with a jingle too
Just like the distances between the earth and sky
Disappear with the light of spirituality.

Notes

1. The month of Chaitra falls between 15 April and 15 May and is part of the spring season in India.
2. The scientific name for the flower malati is *Aganosma dichotoma.* It has jasmine-like white petals and a sharp and pleasant perfume.
3. Navarasas are the nine emotions: love, sorrow, anger, courage, joy, fear, disgust, wonder and peace. Srngara is the emotion of love. The following thirteen verses are an elaboration of the navarasas beginning with love.
4. A story in *Mahapragya ki Kathayen*, volume 3, seems to elaborate on this verse.
5. Avadhi gyan is explained as 'limited supernatural knowledge such as clairvoyance, typical of very advanced ascetics and divine beings' in Agustin Pannikar's book, *Jainism: History, Society, Philosophy and Practice*, translated by David Sutcliffe. This is a knowledge about objects which can be gained even without being in direct contact with them. It does not make use of the senses and is not related to time, space or matter and so is called avadhi according to *Jain Darshan, Manan aur Mimamsa* by Acharya Mahapragya.
6. Brahmaloka is the fifth loka of Devaloka. There are in total twelve Devalokas.
7. Bharata has been mentioned in the earlier cantos. He is the son of Rishabha.
8. Chatak is believed in common lore to yearn for the morning dew.
9. Chakor is a kind of partridge which is said to be in love with the moon and keeps gazing at it all night.
10. In the original consumption it is called 'bhog', and the rhyming word 'yog' is used to indicate meditation or withdrawal from active life or renunciation.
11. Sriyantra is a mandala for auspiciousness and prosperity.
12. Bahubali is a son of Rishabha.

CANTO VI

Risbaha now proceeds to renounce the world, and leaving the city he goes to a park named Nandikar Siddharth. He begins by ridding his body of all its embellishments including the hair on his head. So beautiful was his hair that Lord Indra himself came and stopped him from plucking them out, and as a sign of respect to him, Rishabha let one lock of hair remain. Acharya Mahapragya views this incident as illustrative of the principle of anekanta: even in times of renunciation, it is not your wish alone that matters; concern and compassion for another person's view is just as important. The manner in which a Jain monk pulls out his hair is very unique. They do so with their fingers and this is an important ritual called kesha lunchan. Rishabha does that and then stands in the posture of kayotsarga and looks resplendent.

Of course the people of his kingdom were shocked to hear of his decision to give up everything and lead the life of a mendicant. In a rather piqued manner his followers even asked him why he was against consumption since it brings joy. Rishabha gives a significant reply and perhaps that reply symbolizes Acharya Mahapragya's philosophy of life. He says where there is consumption, it is also necessary to have the knowledge of and practice renunciation—

only then can a society live in balance. It is here that he quotes the example of the sugar cane saying consumption will be sweet only for a while; after that life will be dry and tasteless.

Everyone, including his sons, daughters and wife, plead with him to stay back. The anguished Bharata wonders who would look after Rishabha and to that Kachch and Mahakachch reply that they would be going with Rishabha. Kachch and Mahakchch are representative followers of Rishabha. Four thousand people are said to have followed him and been initiated into the fold.

Rishabha is said to have given advice to his children on how to be a good king and what should be the fundamental principles of governance. One can see the strong influence of socialism in these verses where the stress is on equitable distribution and a society where everyone's basic needs are fulfilled.

Initiation of Rishabha

Born will be a golden dawn
Delighted is the east where the sun rises
As the dawn breaks out on a new morning
Even nature is proud

In the half-open flower is expressed
The flower's full future form
Just as the merit in restraint
Falls within the definition of truth

Behind your back lies Ayodhya[1]
And in front are the Himalayas
Giving up the palace, the journey
to the forests is the unwavering resolve

Lord Rishabha will become a monk
Silent are the emotions of the mind
Of the changing times this is
a hitherto unseen, unknown influence

Just as the wind gives
Movement to fragrance
One man to another in a chain reaction
Is pouring out his heart's content

In the ocean, the waves
Were spreading far and wide
And all this was not visible to the eye
Like the song of a celestial maiden

Dharma, restraint and the monk
Their import is yet unknown
The whole world of words
Is after all a slave to meaning

What will Lord Rishabha do now?
Expectant is the atmosphere
To bring salvation to the world
Is the reason for Rishabha's birth

Hundreds, thousands of people have come
And are standing in front of him
Hands folded, their being in surrender
Everyone's head in humility is bent

Speech is silent, the eyes alone
Said all that had to be
As the wick is by oil fed
Rose the echo of the anhad[2]

Rishabha

You desire that
I keep ruling over the kingdom
You desire that
I keep infusing life into the masses

Respect I do your wishes
But the resolve is to create anew
The mind is set beyond such options
Your desire is thus much in doubt

People's representative

Lord Rishabha remain the king
That organization we welcomed
A time when Rishabha is not king
Is an organization most unwelcome

Organization, new or old
There is not much difference
Where there is your grace
There alone is happiness and bliss

Rishabha

Consumption is increasing
And so is the desire for comfort

There is not a person here, who
can even define sacrifice

It is the character of consumption
To keep increasing along the way
The play of nature is such that
Strife is born with it

People's representative

Consumption is man's nature
Then why do we see strife there?
There is balance proper in nature, then
why this uncalled for anger there?

Misbehaviour or disrespect cannot ever be
the conduct under your shelter
Then what is the reason for writing
This new poem on the merits of sacrifice?

Rishabha

'Excess' always brings with it deformity
In nature, this is the eternal truth
The remedy is to sacrifice the 'excess'
This is the definite truth

We should limit consumption
Restraint is the nectar of dharma

Without knowing the entire truth
Man gets entangled in vain

Emerging from the mountaintop, the waterfall
runs down at great speed
The path if blocked by a cliff
Creates a conflict continual

With the desire for consumption
The eyes have become clouded
To remove this covering veil
The consciousness has to awaken

People's representative

There is pleasure in consumption, why should we,
O Lord, think of it as an illness?
Sacrifice is dry and prohibitive
Alas! How can it be done, O Lord?

Desire we to know
The philosophy of our Lord
And the thought process of
Understanding and realizing your new idea

Rishabha

The sugar cane is full of juice and
Is an embodiment of sweetness

Yet after consumption it is dry
All what is left is a dead stalk

Consumption too while in process
Is sweet and enjoyable
But disenchantment with consumption grows steadily
Its attraction becomes weary

Sacrifice has this unique quality
It is free of excitement in the beginning
But with long years of practice
It brings unequalled sweetness and thrill

The one whose consciousness is awakened
Looks to see the result,
The man who is in slumber deep sees
Only what his passion desires.

People's representative

Darkness removed, the inner being is
illumined with this light
Lord! At your feet salvation we find
Your grace is the protector of truth

The dust of the path which bear your footprints
That path is acceptable to us
For those who on earth do dwell
Nectar is but grain

That which you wish to do, O Lord!
Is what all of us should too

Till today you have lit countless
lights of infinite wisdom

You the creator and the giver
The beginning of all creation
And for social organization,
You alone the base are

Leaving consumption behind, may
we on the path of sacrifice tread
Under the Kalpataru of restraint
May we blossom and flourish

The prayer is spreading silently
Filling the atmosphere
Peace lives in the consciousness
While its search has been in matter

Bharata, do not worry
We are with the Lord
Rose a thousand hands
Of Kachch[3] and many others

With wonderstruck, wide-open eyes,
Said King Bharata,
Is this message of the Lord
For each and every one?

Brother, this a new
Lifestyle
Far away is afternoon
Now it is only dawn

Friends and relatives
Spoke with passion now,
It is difficult to give up home and hearth
As it is for trees to grow without water

Between parallel banks lies
The beauty of the river
Break the bondage of the banks
And it turns avaricious

Kachch-Mahakachch and others speak

Benign is the grace of the Lord
We are filled with gratitude
The wise ones fall in step
with the bestower

Just as water fed to the roots
Turns into sweet nectar in the coconut's womb
Your memory will water our inner
beings with equanimity

Like bees we will partake forever
The honey at our Lord's feet
With abiding devotion
Will flower true detachment

Separated from the city, this
movement is one of new creation
As though the clan is stepping into
A hitherto untrodden path

Following Rishabha, seated on a palanquin was the group
With the force of an ocean
The energy waves of the Lord's mind
Had momentum gathered

By the name of Nandikar Siddharth
The beautiful fertile garden
Became the first place for initiation
Dressed as it was in natural splendour

'Sit down everybody,' came Bharata's
humble request to all
Of different attires everybody, yet
a common creed they shared

The Lord sitting, simple and beautiful,
On the platform of the earth
The rest following him for initiation
Stood in queues in front of him

For kesha lunchan[4] the thumb
and finger are pressed together
As though even the body is
inclined to support consciousness[5]

In the five fistful pulls
One fistful alone was left
Even in the expression of removing the hair
A subtle message was sent

Then came a message, a request from Indra
To leave a clump of hair[6]
Respect for sentiment
Is like beauty seen without any blemishes

Comfortable atmosphere
Standing in the kayotsarga[7] pose
Today the Lord is laying the foundation
Of fulfilment through renunciation

Hands folded, head bowed
The prayer is to the realized one
It was like a conversation between
Beauty and beauty

Total, detached samayik[8]
Is now acceptable to me
Conduct which fosters sin and untruth
Should always be held in contempt

Highest is the sky-kissing
peak of equanimity
Taking place naturally
is a break in the bondage of attachment

Disciples, four thousand, Lord
have been initiated with you
Complete simplicity, life of a monk
To which all of them are new

The Lord, with extra-sensory perception,
With avadhi gyan[9] endowed
Knew the level of the mind and thinking
Of his disciples was but ordinary

The beauty of his consciousness had
Touched the peak of the sahasrara[10]
On the altar of purification of the soul
Was lit an invincible flame

The gift of mahaparyaya gyan[11]
Came to him the first second
The veil of obstruction
Was removed in an instant

With avadhi gyan all knowledge
of the material world
And with manahaparyaya gyan
The minds of all is known

Through the olfactory organ, the sense of smell
recognizes fragrances
Through the world of words, every second
A new meaning is discovered

Free from all bonds
Only liberation is the goal
Given up is consumption
Dharma alone is worshipped

The well-acquainted city of Vinita[12]
Now seems to be becoming unknown
It looked like the people
Were losing their courage today

You are going away, Lord
Leaving us in ignorance
Your guidance helped us distinguish
Between the day and the night

Gaining your shelter, Lord
Even the night was like the day
As your holy feet treads away
Even the day seems like the night

We had the confidence that
The Lord is with us
Why should we worry or fear?
The protecting hand is always on our head

Nurtured we have been in your protection
What will happen now?
What will your solitariness yield?
Lord! This is leaving us with nothing

Blessed by emotions the torrents of
speech were unleashed
With tearful eyes watered
was the whole garden

Bharata wanted to say something,
But tears stopped him
Neither was Bahubali able
Any solution to find

Bharata

O compassionate one, kindly
look at us and make us happy but once
Life and house is a bondage
You being liberated, roam about free

Make this call of devotion
Resounding across the worlds come true
By just saying you will return
Leader, you destroy the anguish of the people

In Bharata's voice, compassion took
the form of a flowing stream
The hearts of the people were overjoyed
And they joined in the chorus

Bahubali

This birthplace is all ours, O Lord!
The beauty of the gardens, of the people, of wealth and fame
Without Rishabha all is empty and hollow
without you there would no cream, O Lord, it'd all be whey

The message of peace will now traverse far and wide
The bee cannot remain far away from the flower
Lord, listen to our prayers, Takshashila[13] is also thirsty
Faith is so strong that our request will not be unheeded

Ninety-eight sons

We too have a right on Ayodhya
It is our birthright
By renouncing, the Lord
has given it up

Detached you, we attached
Tied with tender threads
Free of passion you, we full of it
Are standing in the same courtyard

Remember the Lord
You too try and think of us some time
On your way up or down
Stop for but a second and speak to us

These eyes are full of thirst
Reflecting our inner faith
With every breath of ours
We hear the name of Rishabha

Lord, in our kingdoms too
Do honour us with a visit, we too
will be delighted, like the farmer is
When he sees a pot full of water

The life of a saint like the river
Is a continuous, moving flow
It destroys the sorrows of the world
Erased is unquenched desire

Brahmi-Sundari

The mother of Marudev too was stunned
And stood immobilized and silent
With the trepidation in the hearts of his wives
The earth too trembled

Learned Brahmi and Sundari
Spoke in a trembling voice
Opening the first page of the text
of passion and attachment they said

Lord, when will you return?
Give us some hint
Taking that hint as our command
We too will live every minute

The ears are open, all doors to the
inner heart are closed
In this heart which is full of vibrations
Rare is the one without tremor

Those feet have moved forward
On the call of his goal
Those feet have stayed behind
Lost which are in the world

The bee has learnt to distinguish
And so chose the lotus for a prison
But man has been caught in the prison
of comfort, hoping in futility for happiness

And so amidst natural attachments
The Lord took his first bold step
While among the disciples was
great excitement in the initiation

Predominant was devotion
Little was knowledge
The scene, beyond words
Or understanding

With the feelings of joy and sorrow
We become numb
Beyond this feeling
Lies the bliss of the soul

In the attribute-less soul
They became engrossed
Like water gets completely one
With the body of the ocean deep

Along the banks of the river of bliss
Sat all the groups of disciples
The Lord is taking a dip in it
And a new chapter has begun.

Notes

1. In Jain mythology, the noble people live in Arya khanda and the capital of Arya khanda is Ayodhya. Rishabha ruled over the entire region.
2. Anhad is a sound within the body signifying spiritual growth, especially associated with the awakening of the kundalini.
3. Kachch and Mahakachch were heads of small villages. They have sons called Nami and Vinami. Nami and Vinami were adopted by Rishabha.
4. The process of pulling out hair from the head is called kesha lunchan. It is mandatory for all monks and nuns of the Jain order. The hair is not shaved but pulled out with the fingers strand by strand.
5. The verse says that the pain borne by the body was as though in support of the spiritual desire for furtherment.
6. The story goes that as Rishabha was pulling out his hair, Indra, the voice from the heavens, requested him to retain one clump; he said that that looked better. Rishabha honoured his sentiment and the lesson derived from the story is that it is essential not to be dogmatic about anything and that everything is relative, which is the principle of anekanta.
7. Kayotsarga is a yogic meditative posture, which is also part of Preksha meditation designed by Acharya Mahapragya. Most of the Jain Tirthankaras are depicted in the kayotsarga meditative posture. The word kayotsarga is made up of two words, 'kaya' meaning body and 'utsarga' meaning to give up. Kayotsarga means to give up one's physical comfort and body movements, thus remaining steady, either in a standing or other posture, and concentrating upon the true nature of the soul as being separate from the body.
8. Samayik means to refrain from all activities that can cause you to accumulate karmas. In other words, any activity undertaken attracts some karmic material

to the soul causing it to become impure. So monks and nuns take twelve vows that keep them away from all activities that attract negative karmic particles. Their life is full of samayik. Householders follow samayik each day for forty-eight minutes when they refrain from all such activities.

9. Avadhi gyan: Please refer to note in canto V.
10. Sahasrara, literally meaning a thousand, refers to the 'lotus of a thousand petals', the chakra located four fingers above the crown of the head. The person who practises renunciation is said to be realized when this chakra is activated, for then there is no activity in the brain—no knowledge, no knower, nothing to be known.
11. Mahaparyaya gyan is telepathy.
12. Vinita is another name for the city of Ayodhya as given by Rishabha.
13. Takshashila means literally a city made of stone. It is in this sense that the word is used here.

Canto VII

This canto describes an important day in Jain mythology. It begins by saying how Rishabha was standing in the kayotsarga mudra immersed in his meditation. Looking as though he is divinity personified, he uncovers a new idiom for good life: destruction of the net of desire. He neither eats nor drinks, he neither speaks nor sleeps. He stays still in the kayotsarga mudra for six months. This is too harsh a routine for his followers who wonder how to live and cope. Does a monk have to reach an agreement with hunger and fatigue?

When things reach a point where it is unbearable, most of those who got initiated with him leave. They become what is called tapas sanyasis or mendicants doing penance, and live by the shores of the Ganga.

At that time Rishabha's two adopted sons, Nami and Vinami, arrive and are shocked by what they see. The whole kingdom seems to have turned into mendicants. 'What happened to our king?' they ask. When they realize their king has renounced his kingdom after giving all his sons a part of it, they ask for their share of the kingdom. What will he give, he himself is possessionless, says Dharan or Indra, and he gives them two opposite peaks on the Himalayas as their territory and a celestial vehicle on which they can travel, not to mention the blessing of education. Nami and Vinami are wonderstruck and share their wonder with all the people of Ayodhya.

And then suddenly, after six months, the people find stirrings in the body of the still Rishabha. Excitement runs through them as swiftly as fire in a dry forest. Not only does Bhagwan Rishabha stir, he begins walking towards the city of Vinita. The people are so excited that some ask for a horse or an elephant on which the master may ride. But Bhagwan Rishabha walks barefoot.

Some bring sweetmeats and some bring pearls and precious stones to offer to the Lord, but he partakes of none. Bhagwan Rishabha then goes wandering from place to place begging for alms. For six months he does not get even a morsel.

One night Shreyans, son of King Somaprabha and grandson of Rishabha, has a dream that a black mountain has turned white after it is bathed in milk. Shreyans is an important figure. He is Rishabha's grandson, and later he is the one who incarnates as Mahavira.

In his dream and from his recollection of his past lives, when he sees Bhagwan Rishabha walk into town, Shreyans knows he has to serve the Lord sugar cane juice or ikshu ras. The Lord partakes of that and therefore the race comes to be known as the Ikshvakus. The body that had darkened due to lack of food is now aglow, true to Shreyans's dream.

Acharya Mahapragya also adds a verse where he exclaims on the absence of the sons of Rishabha around him. Perhaps this verse is to highlight the ignorance of the people about how to feed a monk and about monkhood in general.

It is also in this context that Bhagwan Rishabha explains what kind of food may be partaken of so that the adherence to non-violence is complete. One should eat food as a bee draws nectar from a flower without harming it or as a cow grazes on the grass without uprooting it.

The day Rishabha partook of the cane juice is celebrated even today as the day of Akshay Tritiya.

Akshay Tritiya

In the sky of dharma
The sun is rising anew
Awakening is that golden period
Which till now was in slumber deep

Meditating in the kayotsarga[1] mudra
Silence filling the inner self
Divine aura, divine soul
In exaltation they are

Many days have gone by now
But the feet stand unmoving, unflinching, tireless
Gaining victory over hunger and thirst
The inner soul is at peace with itself

Blessed with mind tranquil, experience rich
A new measure is now released
Destruction of the net of desire
Is itself a source of lasting peace

The request of the monks to Kachch-Mahakachch[2]

O Mahakachch! O Kachch!
Shower honey on us all
Becoming a voluminous flow
Cool the heat of this earth

Is this a lifelong agreement
To be signed with hunger and thirst?
Or is there a limit?
Let the answer be a yes or no

With doubt clouding the mind
Ad eager to be assuaged
You are the leading disciples
The first among the rest of us

Under the shelter of hope
Waiting in all humility
What is the lesson that is greater
Than bread in this life?

The answer of Kachch-Mahakachch

First he would teach us
Show us the path
And unwaveringly
His love on us he'd shower

Now silent, the eyes
are half-closed, brother
What to ask? Whom to ask?
That is the problem

If we all go together and the state
of our body and mind describe
Then maybe the knots of anguish
Will unravel

'Yes, hear, hear,'—saying
All the feet moved forward
And came near the Lord
To express their heartfelt feelings

Prayer to the Lord

The feet, the tongue and the mind
Three indicators of consciousness they are
Today the three seem
In variance with consciousness

The feet are eager to move ahead
The tongue is savouring the taste
The mind is restless and thinking
Lord, why this confusion?

What to do for nutrition?
How can we seek pure and sustaining food?
How long will this refrain last?
When will you end your silence?

Lord, hungry we all are
Our throats are dry with thirst
Open your eyes and speak
In your speech lies our faith

In immobility, how will
life move on?
Towards purity of soul and health
Show us the path to both

You are the shelter and we the refugees
To grant refuge is your sacred duty
O embodiment of love that you are,
Recollect those times of old

On one side in the sea of devotion
The boats of the mind were adrift
On the other the plea of hunger
Eager mind and worn out limbs

In a state of hunger, words rob
devotion of its strength
Faith, defeated by hunger,
remains a mere pretence

The feelings of the pupils
couldn't reach the inner mind of the guru
The disciples could not measure up to
the spiritual level desired by the guru

In the presence of a mental distraction
The body's anguish goes away
In which world, anyway,
are all desires ever fulfilled?

From the lotus the honey bee
Can no more nectar draw
Without the sun, the same sweetness
the lotus cannot give

The buzz of the bees around
Has now fallen silent
Who in this world is
by hunger and thirst not beaten?

Thinking together, deciding together

Shall we again go to Ayodhya
And seek shelter under Bharata?
Or should we get caught again
In the family ties we'd given up?

Our thoughts had changed and so we left home
Then why should we go back again?
Let us now, under the open skies
Be free, along the banks of the Ganga

Together they thought and traversed
across the river and along its banks
Cool the shade of the trees
Pure the stream of water

It is easy to eat
Nature's fruits, flowers and leaves
This dance of the river's waves
Are enticing to the mind

The habit of penance
Created the class of ascetics
and thinkers, and philosophy
also matured with them

On the banks of the Ganges
A unique fair was held
In every wave was reflected the
duo: disciple, guru led

Rishabha: The practice of encountering the soul

Alone inside, outside
It was a monologue, Rishabha was silent
The basis of society is the word
And Rishabha's mind had transcended it

There were no desires and the path was laid out
For truth is never in doubt
In the realm of consciousness
No problem is there of likes and dislikes

In the temple of oneness with the soul
The outer world got forgotten
In the atma, in some unknown way
The paramatma was incarnated

Little was the experience of hunger and thirst
The status of a yogi had been attained
Like the light of a full moon night
The lotus-like Lord was in radiant bloom

Standing thus for six months at a stretch
The pace of breathing had slowed down
While active was the consciousness
The outside world created no ripple

Through the inner eye they saw
What was till now unseen
In the practice of equanimity
There is nothing desired or undesired

Inspiring thoughts

This body with matter acquainted
Collects more of it with food
With fasting distance is created
Between matter and its love for more

The gains of the soul unparallelled
Let the meaning of this body be
To safeguard it, and the purpose
of food be to keep the balance right

From the food to the body, and with the body
character and dharma evolves
From character comes human traits
Charting out the beginnings of culture

To only make the body lean
Is to present a one-sided view
Between nutrition and penance lies
The dialogue of anekanta[3]

Charity is not a custom
How will food be got?
There has been no interpreter[4]
There has been no seer

No monk is there anywhere
Unknown is begging for alms
Difficult to get food be fitting a monk
Even if a hundred years go past

Wandering for food

The Kalpataru[5] came alive
Delighted was the earth
With a touch of the holy feet
Every part of it sprung afresh

The earth is experiencing
heaven in its being
The people of the village are excited
Singing devotional hymns they are

Lord Rishabha has come
To his village today
Difficult terrain it is
The Lord's feet were bare

A fine bred horse which can
Run as fast as the mind
Lord, ride it
So they pleaded in pain

Looking wonderstruck
The feet moved on
Unheeded were those words
While the footprints stayed on

Horses are for smaller beings
The Lord is strength incarnate
Go quickly, bring an elephant
Of his stature befitting

Lord, like the elephant Airavata
So strong is this one too
For easy travel on these routes
We desire that you ride it

Please accept this request
We hold devotion in our hearts
Like the large black bees are lotus born
And by nature to it devoted

Knowledge is everything, but
limits of the intellect have to be reckoned with
So while the imagination explored many possibilities
The resolve was firm and unwavering

High-thinking Rishabha
Differs from the masses with narrow minds
Comfortable journey on foot is not a
pain with any regret

A tray full of pearls
Is the gift someone is bringing
Yet someone else in devotion
Is in praise singing

Gold, beads of different kinds
Have been gathered as gifts
For surrender to the worshipped one
Is essential to human nature

So much time has gone past
The Lord has not a morsel eaten
Quickly may I get some ready, so that
the flame of the lamp may burn bright?

There is thirst in the throat
And to quench it water has arrived
And yet in silence it is not partaken of
Everything seems to be asking why

Buttery sweet food items
But not a morsel did the Lord partake
Not even the water jug could get
A touch of his hand

Banned is uncooked food
Boiled food was the kind desired
The focus was unflinching
In the pursuit of non-violence

Bhikshus were visiting
One home after another
But getting alms
Still was a distant dream

The chariot of time
Takes no rest on its way
Days were going past
Even nature seemed detached[6]

Dialogue between Nami and Vinami[7]

When Nami and Vinami came home
One cycle of the journey came to a close
An unfamiliar feeling enveloped them
'Something is amiss' was the feeling they got

Is this our father, or
Is imagination cheating us?
And so they asked, dwellers along the river bank
How did you all come to dwell here?

When the Lord is there, O gentlemen!
How did this orphanage come to be?
This state of being orphaned
How did such a thing come to pass?[8]

Comfortable is the place of residence
Why this uncomfortable shelter then?
We wore cloth made from tree bark
Why have we now abandoned it for wearing bark?

The body is dust-laden
Where is the polish of oil?
The hair that was combed and brushed
with oil, now in tangles is

Bending his head the devoted son asked,
Father, what has happened?
You people who roamed about free in the sky
Are today like parrots in a cage?

Giving everybody a piece of his kingdom
Rishabha himself was in meditation lost
Initiated along with him
We too are fish of the same water

The Lord, hungry even now
Constant movement, didn't stop or get fatigued
We cannot the spiritual path pursue
When suffering from acute hunger

Now to return home, what meaning
would our sacrifice to be forest-bound have?
Given up we our homes
To go back now would be in vain

Man cannot live well
without vegetation is the general opinion
But his penance is based entirely
On spiritual sustenance

Prayer for the kingdom

Master, at the Lord's feet we our shelter seek
He is the one who sees through every event in this world
Firm we are in the conviction that to us also kingdom he will give
With satyagraha our right we will claim

Amazing how to each he has a kingdom given
What mistakes have we committed?
If Bharata is a son, we too are children adopted
Flowers raised in the garden same

Anger, imagination, devotion, combining everything
The two adopted sons came to the Lord's presence
Give us justice! How did you leave us out?
How did the polar star change its position in the sky?

On your order we undertook the journey
Why then did you not give us even a bit of land?
Now end your silence, you benign protector,
Give us all the right to rule. Our dear ruler, reflect!

In vain are the entreaties for a fully bloomed sky-flower[9]
In a second how will the garden of saffron blossom?
Everyday there will be prayer, the kingdom will be got
when watered day after day, the roses will surely blossom

Morning, afternoon, evening, all these times of change
Not one moment went past when prayer was not conveyed
Our mantra for prayer is, give us a kingdom, O King
Lord, you alone make everyone's destiny

To worship at his feet, Nagpati Dharan[10] came
Seeing the devoted pair, he sighed
Who are you and wherefrom have you come, friends
Definitely you have brought an impossible favour to ask

Dharan

The personification of aparigraha[11] he is—
how will he kingdoms give?

Nami-Vinami

Why are you worried,
the blessings of a kingdom we will get

Dharan

You can get the earth from Bharata
Go to him with your request and begging bowl

Nami-Vinami

Who is Bharata? If there is one who gives and we are takers
In this life only the Lord is the deliverer
Listen you, from Bharata we do not kingdom need
This kingdom only the Lord has to give

Dharan

With firm conviction, Dharan then spoke:
'I am Nagaraj, the human form my ascetic robe
Fortunate you are, engrossed in the worship of the Lord
I too am his follower, devoted

The wealth of the Vidyadharas[12] has been gained entire
Arisen has a stream of thought in the mind

This is a rare fruit gained from service to the Lord
A small victory for a group of people with shared belief.'

Saying these words of wisdom, his head he bent
Nagendra Dharan had a new experience
He understood the concept of a religious order now
But who has not, at some time, confronted the intoxication
of power?

Gowri, Pragyapti—the foremost forms of education were imparted[13]
And the twin ranges of the Himagiri[14] was given as kingdom
The education was empowering
For the auspicious mantras were potent

In the creation of the pushpak vimana,[15] the future
looked bright and fortunate
With goose pimples on the body, and the mind elated, the brothers
paid obeisance and took their leave with respect

Look, who is that coming, flying across?
Those engaged in penance saw a new phenomenon
They saw a young man descend from the sky in the pushpak vimana
And wonder tore through the earth like a ray of lightning

Then Nami and Vinami related the amazing event
In his presence, Godliness we felt
The sky wanderers then spoke with delight
And gave king Bharata all the news

Rare are those free from the pride of success
With the strings of the mind man threads his necklace
Bringing their families they came to the mountain ranges
And established kingdoms on the right and left of the Himagiri

Dream of Shreyans[16]

The year took a deep breath of comfort
Faith has found stability
In the outer environment
There is bliss almost like that born of ignorance

The rules of the inner world
Are now becoming known
With multi-coloured imagination
The western sky is a brilliant red

The play of dreams is charming
It is a make-believe world
Even the beggar in a dream
Gains the power of a king

The definition of a dream
The dream itself is making
The dream, like a dancer,
is daily dancing to her own tunes

At the time of realization of the dream
Rages passion like the fire
In it is the hidden message of
deep intense meditation

The golden mountain dark
Is brightened with the abhishek[17] of milk
This dream that Shreyans saw
He drunk as if it was elixir

Who is this lonely man
In this world made of groups and communities?
Do not just see the cream on the milk
There is also butter[18] hidden within

Behind the picture is vibrating
The eternal rule of the unseen
Why does man get entangled only
In the small world that can be touched?

A dream totally unimaginable
The great Subuddhi[19] did see
The mantra of oneness
Was gained by purity

The sun that had been robbed of light
Was once again the source of it
The credit goes to Shreyans
A page of history new

In this chain of dreams being dreamt
One was seen by Somyash[20] too
And thus naturally turned towards
directions known and unknown

The one surrounded by enemies
Today he is the victor
In gaining victory
Shreyans won over even time

In the king's court, quite perchance
All those who had dreamt came together
And were delighted in each other's presence
The rare lotus of bliss bloomed

So Shreyans then told
The story of his dream
Somyash's and Subuddhi's
Stories were similar

They told of their dreams, all three of them
The meaning kept eluding them however
Many were those who these words parroted
Few were those who the meaning knew

The world of words is limited
Meaning is too wide
Without the dignity of meaning
Words are such a burden

The coming of Rishabha to Hastinapur

After relentless travel
The Lord finally to Hastinapur came
He looked a new person
A nomad, but the like hitherto unseen

The beautiful flow of emotions
Entered everyone's hearts
The charming Kalpataru[21]
Bloomed in the yard

Be kind, O compassionate one!
Purify my house
The voice of prayer is beseeching
Fill vibrance in our lives

We are blessed that before us
We have the gem chintamani[22]
We are standing in wait
Just as an empty furnished room

Silent speech, silent skies
Even the lips are unmoving
The definition of truth is difficult
In difficult times too there can be bliss

The moon is in the sky
The ocean takes its reflection
The deafening sound of chatter
Is sending a message clear

How is the whole city today
A collection of verbal felicity?
That was the question of Shreyans
Said the spokesman of the palace

The Lord has to the city come
Like the photosphere of the sun
He glows with sever penance undertaken
And has a brilliant and radiant aura

O the footsteps of the father
Brought goose pimples on the skin
The whole being was excited
The word spread around

The whole family now gathered
In the presence of Rishabha
Worshipping at his feet
The head bowed in devotion

Eyes transfixed, eyelids
had resolved not to blink
At the feet of the liberator
Why close the eyes even for a second?

Shreyans saw him and was completely transfixed
Every moment was like tasting nectar
Seeing his form so
His past to Shreyan's mind came

Arguing and counter arguing
He transcended the mind
In the depths of pure and unwavering
consciousness, he was lost

His memory returned in a flash
The sky became full of light
Accessing the knowledge of his past births
He blossomed like the winter lotus

The Lord was a king
And his charioteer I was
The king's father was a Tirthankara[23]
And one day he said

'The son will be the first Tirthankara
Famous in this world
The exponent of atma vidya[24]
Completely engrossed in bliss.'

At the feet of the Tirthankara
The life of a monk was lived
And followed with great dedication
The lifestyle of an ascetic

To keep the body accustomed to
the tradition of begging for alms
All bondages need be cast away
Should be the focus all along

The festival of Akshay Tritiya

No one knew the method
of giving alms for just maintenance[25]
The hearts of the general public
Was full only with devotion

The requirement of today
Is to adhere to the knowledge gained
May the blessings of prosperity
Make a happy society

To build its nest
The bird collects one straw after another
The holy ones to attain realization
Gather together mantras

Opening is the door which till now
Was closed firmly on the face
New life is being injected into
that which was lifeless till today

Filled with sugar cane
A pot is coming as gift today[26]
The news came immediately
To Shreyans in the market place

Lord, this is unacceptable
Eat something, be compassionate
The pot of feelings is now empty
Fill it with nectar, please

The prayer was accepted
Now the pot in the devotee's hands
Into the cupped hands of Rishabha
poured the juice with devotion

The liquid thickened as it fell
In the shape of a glowing flame
This great example of charity
Became part of the culture to replicate

The sun and stars of the skies
Are giving light to the earth
The gems are in the ocean deep
On the surface is only the boat

The great act of Shreyans
In Hastinapur
Had ripples far and wide
And everyone heard of this act of charity

The day of breaking the fast became
The festival of Akshay Tritiya
The obstacles to sadhna
Were washed away as though with water

Like the veil between knowledge
and ignorance has moved away
Today Rishabha's face glowed
Bondages have broken all

Words of reaction

The cycle of conversation began
Was the Lord not hungry and thirsty all these days?
Who has cast this magic spell
To create such illusions?

Tell me who has food and water
Resisted for so long
Blessed, blessed be Shreyans who
gave him sugar cane juice just now

It is so difficult to remain
hungry for so many days
Even more difficult than that my friend
Is to resist drinking a drop of water

Many problems there are in arduous penance
And yet on the face is a smile
Not to any person in the surroundings
Did he tell of his problems or pain

But what a surprise
Bharata did not heed
that which was gained from his father's feet
Since engrossed he was in kingly pursuits

Even Bahubali was not witness to this
Why was everyone so lax?
Or perhaps the Lord in solitude
Was quiet about his enlightenment

Many citizens spoke in unison
Congratulations, prince! Greetings
to you this day when
you will be very proud

Amazing how this offering of yours
to the Lord was agreeable
No visionary like you
Has your generosity to boast

The Lord gives us affection
Equal to that of a father
With the nectar that flows from his eyes
He satisfies us immensely

We don't know what all has been silenced
He does not ask of our welfare
Broken is the thread of bondage
Lost is his recognition of us

First the Lord was king, now a monk
Changed is his entire stance
He once lived in the outer world
Now he has entered the inner recesses of the mind

In the resolve to follow complete non-violence
How will the horse or elephant be accepted as gifts?
Having given up possession, how would he
Take a gift of gems and pearls?

Like a bee intoxicated with a flower
Partakes of its nectar as much as necessary
But it does not destroy the flower
Which the garden forever keeps

The source of compassion, the Lord
Eats frugally and elegantly like a bee[27]
It is his radiance that
has lit up the inner darkness aglow

The cow eats similarly not uprooting the grass
But feeding off its tips
Not the donkey, who follows no restraint
And uproots the entire plant[28]

One can eat food that
has already been cooked
Surprising why the Lord did not tell us all this
Anyway, now it is all over

With penance his body turned dark
Like sugar cane without juice
That dream of mine has been realized
Dark mountain has been washed white

Hunger and pain have been conquered
The father's dream was realized
Hunger could not tempt him away
The Lord's resolve was strong, unwavering

Dream realized of the great one
The cycle of desire was moving away
Once again with intense introspection
Life was prevented from going awry

Hail! Hail! Munificent one, destroyer of darkness!
Giving new light
Which will radiate in the world
Such faith arises in every mind.

Notes

1. Kayotsarga is a yogic meditative posture as explained in an earlier canto.
2. Kachch and Mahakchch are representatives of Rishabha's followers.
3. Refer to notes in Cantos I and IV.
4. By interpreter it means there has been no one to interpret the texts or the meaning of the rituals, that is, no one to initiate them into the rituals.
5. Kalpataru here refers to Rishabha who is now viewed as the sole provider.
6. The poet is painting a picture of a hallow developing around Rishabha as everything is moving away, even nature. Nothing is unable to quench his thirst or satisfy his hunger.
7. Nami and Vinami were the adopted sons of Rishabha.
8. There is a gap between this and the previous verse in terms of the flow of the story. Nami and Vinami returned from their travels to find their fathers Kachch and Mahakachch, having given up their kingdom, wandering like ascetics in the forest along the banks of the Ganga. So they ask Kachch and Mahakachch: when the protection of King Rishabha is there, why do you behave like orphans? So the poet says it looked like an orphanage where there was no king to protect them. Nami and Vianami wonder what has happened, how this change came to be.
9. The akash pushp or sky flower or kantar kusumvat is an imaginary flower which is said to grow in the sky. It is impossible that a flower grows in the sky. The poet compares it to asking for that which is impossible.
10. Nagpati Dharan was a celestial being. He is also referred to as Dharmendra.
11. Aparigraha, one of the three principles of Jainism, means non-possessiveness. He had nothing he called his.
12. Vidyadharas means celestial beings who are a repository of wisdom.
13. To Nami and Vinami both types of education, Gowri and Pragyapti, were imparted as well as the twin ranges of the Himalayas were given as their kingdom. To traverse atop the hills they were also given a vehicle, the Pushpak vimana.
14. Himagiri means snow clad mountains or the Himalayas.
15. As Nami-Vinami flies in the pushpak vimana, they are referred to as sky wanderers.
16. Shreyans was the great grandson of Rishabha. His father was Somaprabha. His grandfather was Bharata, son of Rishabha.
17. Abhishek is the process by which an idol or a king or great sage is bathed in milk, water, ghee or even with flowers.
18. Butter comes from processing the cream.
19. Subuddhi Shreshti was a rich trader in the city.

20. Somyash was Bharata's son and Shreyans's father. All three of them saw Rishabha in their dreams.
21. Again Kalpataru here refers to Rishabha.
22. Rishabha is referred to as chintamani. The chintamani is a wish-fulfilling jewel.
23. Tirthankara is translated as ford maker.
24. The one who taught about the soul and its existence as separate from the body.
25. The word used here is eshnayut, which means in order to keep the body, the ascetic is allowed to assess with restraint the food available and take only that which is required.
26. Sugar cane juice was the first offering made to Rishabha. It is said this is why he is also known to belong to the Ikshvaku race.
27. A bee takes just that much nectar as it wants and leaves the flower unharmed. This was how Rishabha ate and this is how ascetics are meant to eat. The act is therefore called madhukar.
28. A cow does not uproot the plant whereas the donkey does. Monks and nuns are advised to eat like cows and so their food is called gochar.

Canto VIII

Having broken his fast, Rishabha moves towards Takshashila, where Bahubali is king. He hears that the Lord has come. He is overjoyed and pays obeisance to him mentally, deciding to visit him the next morning. But when he reaches the garden, he finds Bhagwan Rishabha has left. He will not stay in the same place for two nights, the gardener tells him, and another principle of monkhood is laid.

Bahubali however feels cheated. 'Could you not stop him? So many of us are eager to see him,' he tells the gardener. And then he reflects it must have been the night that gave the idea of leaving to Rishabha, uncaring about the disappointments it has caused to so many. Darkness is believed to be the time for all undesirable acts.

Bhagwan Rishabha goes from there to Purimtal, and sits under a banyan tree in the Skatamukh garden. There he delivers this first discourse, after three days of complete fasting. The Samvasarana, as it is called, is held in a beautiful pavilion which is very ornate and elaborate descriptions of it abound in Jain texts. Perhaps that is why Acharya Mahapragya does not dwell so much on the externals as he does on the teachings of Bhagwan Rishabha. He also glorifies the tree as supporting man through life, and even during times of realization.

It is here that he attains enlightenment, and how does that happen? He lives in the moment and is fully alert to every second. He bids farewell to krodh (anger), maan (ego), maya (delusion) and lobh (greed). Crossing these four thresholds he attains kevalya. Kevalya is attained through keval gyana, which means infinite awareness of all substances along with their qualities and variations only accessible to omniscient beings.

Attaining enlightenment

Beautiful nature in the country of Bahali
Glorious, fragrant surroundings
Striking the city of Takshashila
Dignified and respected by all was Bahubali

Green gardens, wide and lush
An aura of joy and peace
Rishabha sits in the pandal,[1] still as a sculpture
Soul, both the ocean and the fish[2]

The king received the good news
Every pore of his body dancing with joy
He jumped up from his throne
His heart full of love and devotion

Folding his hands in obeisance
He spoke with ardour,
Look, O Lord, I am in the palace
See me from where you are

In the morning, along with everyone
I will go, all colours will come alive
As though the rainbow has been willed
For when has permanence alone reigned?

Mingling with light the night went past
Bright and radiant was the dawn
Bahubali sitting on the elephant
Heart engrossed at the feet of the Lord

Power has its own form
Obedient, abiding family
It was as though enthusiasm had been personified
And everyone's desire had the right direction found

Opened were the doors to the garden early
Where is Rishabha? Asked everyone
In a voice wonderstruck, the gardener
spoke with hands cupped bud-like

Lord will not (from the same place) see two sunrises
And so to catch sight of this gem is not easy
Just as the sun roams[3] the sky
This sun-like human roams the earth

Is it true that the Lord has set out to travel?
Why did you not stop him?
O you the one who is the base for the baseless
What is this distasteful behaviour?

Everyone thirsting for but a view
is waiting, not even blinking the eye
What is this you have done, good grief!
Is darkness spilling into light?

How many dreams, how many feelings
How many types of thoughts?
Who will hear, O compassionate one
You were always merciful to me

What is this work so essential?
Could you not take two days rest?
Here or there, you have to meditate
Was this garden not good enough space?

Detached Lord, you are not to blame!
It is the dense darkness that is at fault
Darkness has spread its net around me
I am not able to pay obeisance at his feet

Lord, how will there be assurance?
When faith itself cheats on you
The mind did not entertain doubt
That we will not be able to you sight

The Lord in Takshashila
Has not partaken of any food or drink
This is an insult to us
After all, we too have a heart, dear Lord

The compassionate cry of Bahubali
Made the mind overflow with empathy
Said the sweet-tongued secretary Sudhir
Why, O King, are you so vulnerable today?

The Lord Rishabha's stay in Takshashila
Has not quenched our desire to behold him
This is the root of all sorrow
And the mind goes through emotional turbulence

How can the Lord, seated in the heart, be far from us?
Like the sun appears everywhere on earth though far away
Distances of near and far disappear
Lord, you have made this happen

Why then is your lotus face sad?
Why is faith wilting?
In every breath the Lord lives
And the sky stands witness to this bliss

Like the rising bubbles of the boiling milk
The words of the secretary gave energy
Bahubali now happy within
Got back to his palace home

Journey and coming to Ayodhya

Glory to the Lord, travel continuous
Over a thousand years across different lands
Practising silence, meditation strong
Naturally is the unseen coming to be seen

In the outskirts of the city of Purimtal
Like a tilak on the forehead of Ayodhya
Was the garden of Shakatmukh
Glorious and vibrant in the east

Under the banyan tree, the base attractive
Its many branches very beautiful
Seeing the Lord sit in its shade
Wrote nature an epigraph new

Man was inseparable from the tree
Between them affection grew
Man even attained salvation because of the tree
The tree too extended a helping hand

Man loves trees
Trees are the basis of his life
Becoming the stimulus for enlightenment
Gentle leshya,[4] gentle conscious mind

City dwelling created a distance from the tree
Established a difference between man and nature
Near the man-made house of comfort
The tree stands as the source of faith

Under the banyan tree the Lord lived
The never-dying light of knowledge
For three days he fasted
And rested in his soul's abode

The new experience of mindfulness[5]
How spectacular the inner being!
Rejecting the suggestions of the senses
A new world came to view

Where matter is purely for knowing
Behind the veil lies the reason
Nothing is without a cause
The soul is the knower and the soul is knowledge

There the ego protests wildly
And pleads with the intellect
Why do you awaken today
the sleeping lion, O Adhiraj!

If total bliss is awakened
You will be left without a ripple
Life will lose its allure
The ego will become a burden

You speak the truth, son of man
You have the secret for understanding truth
Friend, not within my control
is to awaken knowledge pure

My territory has been transgressed
My inner eye has been opened
Wisdom has its own lands
Barred is the entry of the ego there

Go seek shelter elsewhere
Blessed will you be and independent
The outside world is everyone's base
The doors to which always open are

Rising in status

Anger! Friends! Listen and accept
Search out your own places
Maya! Goddess! Listen to this announcement
Kindly, quickly make your way

Friends! Greed! A place that is desirable
Search it out and relax
Give up, all of you, my company
In acceptance may hands rise

What has happened today, O master?
You are giving up everybody yourself
We are all friends with you
This decision is very strange

We implore you please think again
Our logic should be acceptable
Will the one with no beginning have an end?
How will autumn turn to spring?

Anger was in full form
The inside being was also very passionate
The ocean heaved with a big wave
As though boiling milk had been topped with salt[6]

Patience and courage though subtle in form
Said, 'Friends, we were not present earlier
We live in pure hearts
Do not argue, change your attitude'

Anger was silenced
Ego and arrogance changed their form
Maya became removed from existence
And yet greed remained seated

Did not see any friend here
Everyone has gone beyond
In aloneness there is no exuberance
And so he took to his path

The fearful chieftain of the senses is delusion
Everyone has his net of illusion
Finished was the inner conflict
The inner being was now free of duality

The consciousness of detachment now developed
There was dazzling light emanating from all directions
Without a single wave was the ocean today
The lotus blooming with the rays of the sun

All veils were removed
There remained not a mark within
All source became the source of the chitta[7]
From every atom brilliance was exuded

Brilliant is the network of the rays of light
Fragmented has become whole today
That which was unknown has now become known
Sentient-insentient, all knowledge separate

Like a berry in the hand, everything was apparent
The examples of matter and its many manifestations
The relation between word and meaning
Leaving behind no explanation unknown

Rose the boon of keval gyana[8]
The amrit kalash[9] of nectar filled
Man can be omniscient
The rest of life is a fleeting rainbow

Flooding the word with comfort and joy
Barred are not the doors of hell
The meeting of atma and atma
From Adinath,[10] this union was born

The sensory mind came to a grinding halt
The inner being was active without a pause
Sounds silenced, experiences fully known
Only the mystery of kevalya[11] unknown.

Notes

1. This pandal was known as samavasaran.
2. When the poet says the soul is both the ocean and the fish he means it is both inside and outside; everything is in consonance with the soul, there is no external aspect. In Jainism, to live in harmony in the soul is the ultimate goal and Rishabha achieved that state.
3. Rishabha is likened to the sun. The verse says that he will not stay in the same place for two consecutive days. Just as the celestial body sun roams across the sky, so does Rishabha roams across the earth.
4. Leshya is a specific term in Jainism that is used to broadly mean the mental attitude.
5. Mindfulness means being alert and in the present.
6. The wave which is generally on the surface of the ocean. This time it was an upheavel, the whole ocean surged forth. The poet compares this to the froth of boiling milk which had further been topped with white salt.
7. The conscious mind.
8. Keval gyana is the infinite awareness of all substances along with their qualities and variations only accessible to omniscient beings.
9. Amrit kalash means a pot of nectar.
10. Rishabha is also called Adinath or the first Lord.
11. Kevalya is the attainment of keval gyana.

Canto IX

This is a touching account of how Marudev, Rishabha's mother, suffers. She is filled with anguish that her son is roaming in the forests, barefooted and alone. When Bharata asks her why she is unhappy, she says only a mother's heart will understand and continues to talk a little angrily with him.

It is then that they hear Rishabha has come to town. He is being attended upon by not just humans but also celestial beings. As mentioned earlier, there are four gatis or states of existence according to Jain texts: naraki or those who live in hell, tiryancha or animals, plants and similar beings, manushya or human beings, and deva or heavenly beings or those who access a better life living in luxuries and comfort and occupying the highest rung in the ladder of existence. The soul is reborn in one of the four categories depending on one's karma. Living beings of all the four states had assembled around Rishabha.

Mounting an elephant Bharata and Marudev go to Purimtal. When she sees her son glowing and wise, calm and serene, Marudev's joy knows no bounds. The joy opens doors for kaivalya and the first one to attain moksha right there is Marudev. It may be pertinent to add here that even though mythology has chosen to begin with Rishabha, they themselves recollect many of their past births and deeds making the beginning, as they claim, without any specific point in time. In each birth, according to their actions, they move to a higher birth. The progress is slow since good and bad karmas add to one's progress. In the case of Marudev, however, she was a nigodh or the lowest form of life—her soul was in the body of a common plant. From that she was reborn a woman and then she attained moksha. In between all this Bharata's armoury guard comes in with a piece of news that portends the events to come. Bharata has become Chakravarti or emperor because the chakri ratna has appeared in his armoury. An interesting choice eloquent of life is what Bharata faces: about what should he rejoice more—the weapon, or his father who has given up all arms?

Thereafter, the canto elaborates upon the characteristics of the soul.

The theory of the soul

With auspicious recitations the early morning began
Stretched itself awake
The celestial vehicle of the sun, spread out
Becoming the seat of everlasting light

All the ten directions laughed merrily
The wind, the messenger of fragrance became
The branches moved, swayed about
And the trunk still, stood firm

With the first ray of light King Bharata
Came in the presence of Marudev
As he looked up from her feet above,
He saw her face, with eyes closed in meditation

Mother, look! Your grandson
has come to celebrate his position
In this happy time when the lotus is blooming
Why is there any worry?

Who? Bharata! Yes, mother I am
And you ask why worry, my son?
It is like asking this room in the palace
When you are enclosing space within, why this window?

Bharata, worry you do not have
Who in arrogance have closed the windows
She alone will worry whose
children roam the forest

Do you any idea have where Rishabha is?
What does he partake of for food?
Winter, summer, how he bears?
How he survives each day?

Remembering those days am I
When feed him I would with my hands
Serving him myself,
I was the lamp, I was the wick

The taste of food, with mother's love
added to its relish
Natural winds and that from the handfan
Both would warm the heart together

How beautiful were those days
Bharata, you are witness yourself
of times when life was full of fun and charm
And eyes danced in joyous glee

Today he is alone, who else is with him
as witness to his joys and sorrows?
In olden days they walked on foot
Today, the elephant everyone mounts

His feet are bare
the path rocky and uneven
scorching earth, scorching sand
even the sun shines mercilessly

The earth is bed and blanket too
how can one draw sleep then?
The night must be keeping awake
as though memory into forgetfulness fades

Bharata, the fault is not yours
When did Rishabha remember you?
Even once, however small,
A message did he send to you?

Tears in the mother's eyes
Sons become cruel
Forgetting her care and nourishing
Growing wings, fly off they do

Walking behind the calf is the mother
A mother is always a mother, dear
In the initial years of a new life
She alone is the protector

It is not right that worry for me
rests on your head, Bharata!
Child, may your heart be happy
And full of joy your household be

Thus with blessings from his grandmother
The king to his palace came
Somehow the mind is chuckling
As it senses the festive spirit in the air

Within the heart, consciousness sprouted
Awakened was the faith in the soul
Success means becoming one with the goal
And this portends a future bright

Two pleasant to hear
Hitherto unheard messages came
As though religious texts had been
explained on the anvil of materialism

The gardener

In the garden of Shakata, in the town of Purimtal,
Lord Rishabha has arrived
Assembled are man and celestial beings
Innumerable as the stars in the sky

Rose animated conversations about the Lord
Who has attained keval gyana[1]
A divine pavilion, wonder creation, they made
The samavasaran, a celestial vehicle, as though descended

The armoury guard's news

Glory to the emperor! Glory be to him
The celebration of victory has drawn nigh

All by chance in the armoury
has appeared an amazing weapon, the chakra ratna

Divine light of radiant source
A network of rays sparkling
Glowing brilliantly is the armoury
Putting an end to all chaos

The mental state of Bharata

Delighted in every pore of mind and body
Joy abounding in pride arose
Like the small baby eagle
Eager to fly on its newly sprouted wings

Between two options
The king has to choose
First whom should I bow to?
The subtle remains the root of the gross

Message from the water carrier

The maid carrying water to the inner chambers
Came to Marudev
Mother, today we saw
A gleaming sky with a brilliant halo

Marudev

What, where, who has seen this?
Wonder is writ in every aspect of nature
Has Rishabha come? The minds of
the people of Vinita are now filled with hope

The water-carrier woman

The master is a yogi
With a halo around his head
Brilliant he is, resplendent he is
Indeed, the king of kings

A cliff now adorned as the throne
Gloriously ornamented the umbrella
Mother, wonder of wonders!
The whole garden has become green

In every particle beauty nestles
Inviting, attracting everyone
And the people are now saying,
Today has come a different Lord of Ayodhya

Blooming with joy the mother's face
The lotus-like eyes shone with joy anew
Worry gave way to happy thoughts
Removed was all anxiety

Every second of eagerness, was each
longer than a year by far

This is an experience of relative truth
That which is short, is also long

Rishabha has come, Rishabha is here
The inner mind started to cheer
Emotion and language came together
Unknowingly in expression

Fervent was the desire to be in his presence
But how to imagine him? A picture was lacking
When the transformation of the past into future
is visible, only then the mental picture would be complete

And then a voice unheard hitherto
Assured that one should not about anything worry
For today in the courtyard of Ayodhya city
The Lord, brilliant as the sun, has come

Come on, let's go and see the Lord
Mother, look! The elephant is ready
Heavier than the mountain Mandhara
Is the cost of reprimand[2]

In a state of happiness
Mother placed her hands on Bharata's head
Awakened was the experience of the subconscious
As a pot is full of nectar

With every descending step of the ladder
Came an equal increase in joy
Often in descent there come
rare moments of ascent

As step after step they hurried to the outskirts
The city of Ayodhya never seemed so large
For after all, the body traverses only at a certain speed
While the mind gushes forth unbound

Coming close to the samavasaran
Said the humble Bharata with folded hands,
Mother, see! There Rishabha is seated
Splendorous he is as you would desire

Saw the mother the omniscient's glory
The cloud of wonder became intense
Himself unadorned but surrounded by
brilliant presence,[3] looks like he is engrossed

Broken was the fearful illusion
On seeing the situation different now
The picture of strife that she had sketched in her mind
Was now a figment of imagination

In the piquant voice of reprimand
Bharata's ears were still resounding,
Said Marudev, 'In every bead of memory's necklace, my fingers
have unknowingly prayed as a rosary

How was I to know that Rishabha is in the vicinity
Was seated in such splendour
I thought he was a forest-roaming wanderer
An emperor[4] he has come to be

How brilliant is the aura of his face?
How glowing is his body's vermilion hue?
Glimmering they are, glowing they are
Like freshly sprouted leaves on every branch

So many days have I been weighed down
by the futile burden of worry
Eloquent in his visage is the truth that
asceticism is no burden, but a blissful gift

Seeing am I without blinking
He is in himself engrossed
The mother's mind confused with love
A neutral, stoic son, no longer immature

Woe to my thoughts born of love
The unfettered one experiencing the supreme
In detachment the mind finds oneness with the soul
The one who learns this sutra is for ever successful'

With oneness is erased the difference
between contemplation and the one who contemplates
In just a second the mother grasped the sameness between
the all-knowing and the experience

Marudev, awaken, awaken lady
You have been sleeping for endless time
Deep sleep, intense delusion
Awaken to spring for the first time

Hailing and to oneself awakening
Being one's own mirror, one's own reflection
Wondrous it is to behold maya
The sun in the sky and reflection in the water

Hastening, quickening she went forward
Selecting the ascetic fold
Detach she did from the world, became she a kevali[5]
Choosing her soul for her nourishment

Body, so long you have been with me
As speed with a horse rests
Speech! Mind! Keep away
Voice divorced from thought

The first contact of voice
The first vision in the mind
Mother, I could become of Adinath
A human body I could become

Today I take leave
To the left and right of me do not tarry
Mind! Speak! Speak my voice!
Long-time companion, my body, bear this

In a motionless state the mother
Became liberated from bondages
Now she will not knit spider webs[6]
In her own power she rests

Said Rishabha, 'Mother Marudev,
This is the moment of attaining siddhi'
Freed from tradition, the voice of dharma
Spoke in every word of the Lord

The ears are attentive, the eyes are open
But everyone is dumbfounded
As though thought has become thoughtlessness
And inner conflicts have been arrested

What a loss! Truth the eyes have beheld
Mother seated on the elephant
Indeed, Rishabha's words were not false
An unprecedented event has come to be

Moving forward, stopping and moving again,
Bharata went towards his grandmother
Marudev became immortal in death
It re-emphasized his faith

Performing the last rites, they all
reached the presence of Rishabha in bliss
Then flowed from the Lord's mouth
The gushing river of sagely wisdom

Body and soul, two truths are
The body mortal, the soul immortal
The body is born and it dies too
The soul, always eternal, immortal

Listen, listen! Alert yourself
to this new message pure as the waterfall
Hidden is our refuge
Alluring is the unknown land

The soul is truth, beauty divine
A blessing auspicious
It is a gift of the higher consciousness
And the method to get there is through restraint

Subtle truth it is and so
Sometimes attainable, sometimes not
But the consciousness is with everyone
Naturally beautiful and worthy of adulation in every being

'I am' this experience tells
The existence of the soul immortal
One who lives for even but a moment
Has always lived, his existence can never be erased

Sentience remains the sentient
No empathy with insentience it has
Between the sentient and the insentient
There lies a natural and increasing chasm

Five senses as five subjects
Have taken form in this world
But the sentient soul is formless
And its quest our engagement

Matter takes different forms
Of which we learn through the senses
The infiniteness of the sky, for instance,
How much of it can be measured by our eyes?

In the strength of un-clading
Lies the chance to know the soul
Realization or personal experience
may also cause its appreciation

In the waters of the mighty ocean
Rise and fall the waves with ease
In destiny's cycle of rebirth
The soul is of different hues

The greatest sutra for attraction is how
to keep the wick burning, how to draw the oil
So too does every action
attract karmic matter to adhere to the soul

The wick keeps drawing oil
This the sutra for attraction great
Every action attracts and
matter becomes the karmic design

Karma, action and rebirth
Have a special connection with the soul
On these four should be based
All of human conduct

Human conduct should be
Based on non-violence
The one who after destroying peace and sowing
seeds of sorrow laughs—that is violence

From this downpour of the water-laden clouds
Bathed were all the learned men
The darkness of the moonless night
was dispelled with glowing light spreading far

The inner felicitous voice
Rose in resonance across the skies
Impenetrable joy, new hopes and
peaks to conquer, new light shines anon.

Notes

1 Refer to note 8 in Canto VIII.
2. Bharata was reprimanded by his grandmother that he did not care about Rishabha. So heavy was that reprimand that he was here to take his grandmother to meet Rishabha.
3. Many celestial beings were said to be present all around Rishabha.
4. The word emperor is used because Rishabha later describes the world of the renunciate as the true empire, where a king is never challenged and so he never loses his kingdom, for the kingdom is within him. So Marudev saw him as an 'emperor: king of kings'.
5. The one who has attained keval gyana is a kevali.
6. Meaning she was free from the cycle of births and rebirths.

Canto X

The mood changes and now from a world of non-violence we are transported to Bharata's kingdom. Mythology says that when a king is blessed, the heavens shower gifts on him. The title chakravarti, which is given to an emperor, is bestowed upon him by the chakri or the wheel which has enormous powers.

This canto describes the kind of powers King Bharata got as a result of all the thirteen ratnas he was blessed with. The powerful wheel, or chakri, gives him and every king the title chakravarti. We also see the arrival of the thirteen ratnas or gems. They are called ratnas because they are the best in the category to which they belong. The chakr, dand, chatra and asi were born in the armoury of the king. The senapati, grihapati, vardaki and purohit were born in the residential quarters of the king. The charma, mani and kakini were found in the king's treasury. The ashva (horse) and hasti (elephant) were the five sensory ratnas. The mani ratna is said to be found on the forehead of the elephant. Then there was also the stri ratna, the woman designed to please the king (!).

The senapati was the leader of the community and was adept at conquering countries beyond the Ganga and the Sindhu. The grihapati managed the household of the king. The purohit worked to appease the stars and the planets. The elephant and the horse were endowed with great speed and courage, and the elephant had the mani ratna on its forehead. The vardaki worked in the field of construction and was the one who built the bridge over the rivers Unmagn and Nimagn across which the king's army marches. Stri gave great joy in lovemaking. The chakr was the best of all weapons and was capable of gaining victory. The chatr, on gaining the touch of the king, became twelve yojanas in length and breadth and was specially made with different metals. Many symbols were inscribed on it and it could protect one from sun, shade, rain, etc. The charma beneath the twelve yojana-long chatr could grow crops in a single day. Mani was embedded with gems and had six parts. It was located between the chatr and the charma. It could shed light up to twelve yojanas and helped in entering the dark cave. On the human body it could destroy all illnesses and keep everlasting youth. Kakini was made of gold and it could wipe out darkness where even the sun, moon and fire could not. Khadag was unparalleled in strength on the battlefield and it never missed a target. Dand had five branches embedded with gems and it could destroy all enemies and fulfil all the wishes of the king. Through a special practice it could even funnel through 1,000 yojanas below the earth.

While the number of ratnas mentioned in the poem are thirteen and the *Tanam* gives fourteen, it could be because the chakr has already been mentioned in the previous canto or it could be because the horse and the elephant have been grouped together. The poem says the kakini ratna was able to throw light up to a distance of one yojana. One yojana is an ancient measure of length/distance. The exact measurement is disputed among scholars with distances being given between 6 to 15 km.

In this canto, Bharata sets out to conquer other lands as these gifts inspire him to do. It may be worth mentioning that he is a king and the duty of a king is to expand his area of influence. So his desire to annexe neighbouring kingdoms is well received. He wages many wars. Described here is his war with the mountainfolk.

He attacks the mountainfolk and they being fiercely independent, fight tooth and nail. Finally, they pray to their god who himself descends and tells them that to fight the chakri is not wise. Even though he suggests a compromise, the struggle of the human mind to accept compromise is explained beautifully before it finally succumbs—a compromise is the only way when the opponent is the blessed one. In this case Bharata was predetermined to be the chakravarti and the gods had given him the all-powerful chakri; its will cannot be opposed.

Conquest of the world[1]

Today all the world around
Shakti, you are being worshipped
You, the root mantra for all-round success
Invigorating is any discussion on you

Vibrant with your thoughts is the mind
Filled with your thoughts speech is ever flowing
In every movement of the body it is you
Auspicious and beautiful

On the seat of knowledge and
meditation, you are at the fore
In every part of sky and space
Is impressed your picture

Ambitious man enforces his
power over others
Like the dodder plant, a parasite he is
Who lives off others' powers

For the strong man, the weak one's fears
become his wealth to tap
Devi, then you are not able to remain the
universal mother with love for all

Your seat of authority is in
weaponry and the muscular strength of men
Blessed by you that person is
loved by everyone

King Bharata to offer prayers
to the armoury went
There the chakra ratna's aura shone
Resplendent as a youthful maiden

He circumambulated thrice, as a humble
pupil would his beloved teacher revere
Shakti is the highest Lord's master
As the waterfall from the mountain flows

Going down on his knees, left knee first
And then the right he bent to touch the floor
Before the chakra, Bharata looking
every bit a new ascetic born

Folding his hands in obeisance, the King
Bharata said in a voice so sweet
Chakra, your limitless strength
Which man has ever measured?

Opened you have the door to victory
You invincible, fearless one
How can anyone disregard you?
You benevolent, auspicious one

Having worshipped the chakra, the king
came to his residence own
The brilliant streaming rays of the sun
now sang the sweet song of victory

The power of the chakra gave expression
to the strength of the ruling king
Just as with paternal tenderness flows
life in the newborn child

In the auspicious time of bhagyoday[2]
All the ends do meet
Just as all the stars come together
In the horoscope of the great

Two-tusked elephant, horse, sword, gems and the kakini ratna[3]
The pundit, the divine and the army
Thirteen wondrous gems came together
By fate, the natural scientist

Born was the inspiration to conquer the world
The euphoria created by the chakra shakti
The unparalleled play of destiny's appointed hour[4]
Is a gift of creation itself

The chakra ratna moved forward
Easily travelling across the skies
Like the sun who brings light to the world
And is a wanderer in the sky

With the danda ratna, the horse-mounted
chief of armed forces is fearless
To be a follower is a very
rare engagement in life

The chief priest to bring peace
Now took full control
For just one cup of nectar can
make poison ineffective

Daily need for food and drinks
was the grihi ratna's onus
The wondrous powers of the divine
Is like the lightning in the sky

Working overtime to meet
the daily requirements of shelter
was the ratna vardaki
So regarded as the yogi of the times

Charma ratna could feed the entire
army for days and days together
Under the chatra ratna's protection from rain
and shine, the charma ratna would function

Together the different ratnas and the kakini ratna
were as brilliant as the sun
Night began to look like day
So dazzling was the illumination

Marching ahead with the trail of ratnas
Desiring to conquer the world was he
Even after getting everything, the human mind
remains every minute for more thirsty

He conquered all of Magadh
Across the Ganga and the river Sindhu
When fate supports, then effort
gets strength immediately

Pronounced was the king's decision
General, march you to the state
Near the river Sindhu go forth
And blow the bugle of victory

Charma ratna will be your boat
The river is thus no problem
Where the celestials are forever present
Penance always brings result

It is in the shape of the srivats[5]
With the crescent moon engraved on it
Steady, unmoving, impenetrable as a shield
It throws the enemy in a quandary

For farming the lands are fertile
Sow early in the morning
Evening harvest and eat to your heart's content
At night sleep deep and peaceful

Taking to heart the king's orders
He came to the river bank
Taking the charma ratna
In humility did he bow in obeisance

To the other end of the river
Charma ratna became the boat
What a rare occasion this, when
earth's firm ground was on water felt

Thus the chief took the army
easily to the other shore
Even the shore appears to draw closer
When the one approaching is powerful

In the short-lived battlefield
The army conquered easily
The residents of the snow-clad mountains
Recognized the force of destiny

Hands folded in humble salute,
Said the chief of army softly,
'Order us, Master! All are ready
To go southward, shall we?'

Well done gentlemen, march ahead army
Measure your muscle strength
The cave of darkness is too black
Go ahead and gain entry into it today

Master, fulfilled will be your desire
The danda ratna, defying verbal
description, is famous for
fulfilling every heartfelt desire

In a second, undulated terrain
evens out as plains
Valleys disappear seemingly
And ditches close up

So the chief of army staff
saluting, lifted the danda ratna
Humility, the first mantra of success is
He sought it and got it

Seeing the cave's black and
frightening shutter, in spite
of total faith in the danda ratna
The human heart hesitated

Thus teasing the invisible,
strong warrior sitting within,
he asked, 'Why hesitate? Power is in hand
Take courage, the most potent arm'

Awaking as the dawn, the light of bravery
Rose in pure, unstinted brilliance
Danda ratna revelling in the sky
was frightening celestial beings

Paying obeisance and then circumambulating
He caused the mountainous door to fly aside
Like a saint in still meditation
Brightly opening his eyes

Accomplishing all his tasks the army chief
Gave him all tidings of joy
King Bharata's mind danced
As in a garden in spring

The divine ratna mani[6] was presented
Brilliantly shone the elephant's forehead
Lightning struck and thunder roared
Resounded songs of praise

The one on whose forehead it is
To him old age does not come
Hair, nails and skin remain young
Surprising indeed—who has measured the sky?[7]

Fearless, unruffled the mind becomes
And diseases does not annoy
In the battlefield the enemy's
weapons would be of no avail

Undisturbed by the nuisance of divine or beast
The mind would be ever joyful
The ever-flowing stream of the waterfall
Would tell the story of progress

Kakini ratna, of all-pervading brilliance
And an eternal source of light
Immeasurable power to counteract poison
That even ambrosia is its slave

Of four sides and shaped like an anvil
With petals eight holy
Blessed indeed is the earth
Bearing such powerful ratnas

Intense blackness, pervading darkness
Darkness even the sun can't drive away
And the full moon with its silvery light
Would still this night not be able to illumine

The kakini ratna each of those
dark particles would render brightly lit
Adding its touch as a diamond it would
change the very form of light

In the dark cave the chakri[8]
took steps forward
With the might of the kakini
every strain shone in radiance

Forty-nine divisions came to light
Lighting one yojana[9] at a time
This unique sphere of sun-like light
As a way to remove darkness and night

Each division of one yojana
And the number of yojanas increased
As though the night were no longer estranged
With the sun every bit was like day time

Two streams, Unmagn and Vimagn, between their banks
Were awe-inspiring in their flow
As though telling a new story of
surfaces and depths hidden within.

The vardika ratna made in a second
A bridge across the river
Crossing the river, the army secretively
brought Bharata to the river shore

Troubled by the shower of arrows
By the mountainfolk,[10] the army turned away
Powerful inspiration is independence
That can break through even a snake's hold

The army taking the khadag ratna[11]
Conquered all in a stroke
And they retreated, fleeing as a deer
would on catching sight of a leopard

How amazing is the strength of the mind
Like water that turns into pearl
Defeated they were by the army
And yet defeat they did not accept

The sandy shores of the river Sindhu
Dried the sweat drops of the struggle
And droplets of the desire for victory
Came together as an ocean

Freedom is our birthright
We will not become slaves
Constant and steady in our resolve
The garland of victory we will wear

O Kuldeva![12] This is the right time
for you to give us all your support
The one who does not gauge the value
of time, sick he becomes

Becoming a devotee so prayed the leader
And gave up food and drink
Three days in constant remembrance
Difficult life he lead

The coming of Deva Meghmukh

Vibrating with the waves of his reflection
The Deva Meghmukh[13] came
Tell me why you thought of me, he asked
Why does your face and form lack lustre?

The prayer of the mountainfolk

Thirst there is in our parched throats
Send down the torrential rain
Dried up is the beautiful garden
Do bring it to life again

Without strife was our territory
The land fertile and peaceful
We don't know who and from where
has come to destroy our peace

On this holy land the feet of
no enemy should be able to stand
Every grain of sand on this land
Resound with the call for freedom

That there should be such a possibility
This the only prayer
The one who came as a conqueror
May he leave hungry and thirsty

Deva Meghmukh

In the courtyard of love stretched across the sky
Echoed the divine voice
That task which is well timed
Will reap desired results

This chakri is the master of six regions
And the king of the devas
Take instructions and surrender to it
Follow the only path

It cannot be defeated by man or divine
Read the language of destiny
The one who knows not the rules of the world
Fosters hope and despondency

Mountainfolk

Woe! The penance will bear no fruit
And the effort will be in vain?
Will the presence of the worshipped Deva
Not bestow upon us any gain?

Eyes filled with tears and speech soaked
Compassion drew in all other emotions
Every cell of the trembling body
Even in silence was eloquent

Deva, the feeling of amity
would be full of secret meaning
With the support of just one sutra
Man prays on the rosary

With divine power, even the impossible
becomes possible
What kind of friend are you?
Upholder of the enemies

Deva Meghmukh

My devoted one, your joy is precious to me
Why are you getting upset?
I nurture the undifferentiated
Why are you seeing differences?

The fire knows the value of wind
What will the bee know?[14]
What do hurtful words know,
for instance, of the beauty of desire?

May your flower[15] of independence
Bloom and blossom for you
Becoming wind, spreading its fragrance
Blessed will be your act

Rains showered by Deva Meghmukh on chakri ratna

Naturally the sky became filled with
dark, foreboding clouds
Glimmering, glistening, the lightning
showed its flash of brilliance

Heavy, pelting torrential rains came down
The army was taken by shock
Who has ever written the story
of upheaval in the army?

Water everywhere on the earth was flowing
The chariots looked like boats
Horses and elephants had to swim
In this attack without weapons

Just with the touch of the chakri
The charma ratna an island turned
The chatra ratna formed the roof
And the gem (mani) became brilliant as the sun

The grihi ratna grew crops
All problems were solved
And thought everyone in this instance,
Whose penance was paying off?

Bharata's thoughts

Who is the unfortunate one
Who tried to turn the wheel of destiny?
Who is the one creating this illusion
And suddenly sending down rains?

In the mental state of Bharata
The divine became partner
In the complete power brought by danda shakti
The emotion of anger arose

Said man in passionate rage,
O! What is this Meghmukh
You had the audacity to try
and challenge the chakri?

Move, move, if you want to be well
And go your way home
If you want to fight, then arm yourself
and present yourself

All at once the clouds retreated
The outer space turned bright
When destiny wishes you good fortune
Then even the earth becomes fertile

He, Meghmukh, kept his word as a friend
How long can the cloud weave
the shroud of darkness
against the sun?

O young mountainfolk, you will succeed
Now listen to my advice
on how to get that victory
Don't continue to be adamant

Seven days of very hard work
—has it borne fruit?
Did the cloud needlessly collide
with the sun's net of light?

The inhabitants of the mountains

The inherent attraction in the magnet
Draws iron to itself thought the vanquished,
And wondered, who is the supporter of the weak?
Who is the deliverer of the defenceless?[16]

Our very own Lord, how he played
to the gallery! No surprise this
For who has ever measured
the grief of the powerless?

We just have to surrender, we have no choice
So they began to think
Together, they all came to the other side
And surrendered to Bharata

Having gained the promise of self-rule
The mountainfolk were pleased
Shone they all did in the moonlit environs
As brilliant, hallowed stars.

Notes

1. This canto describes the kind of powers King Bharata got as a result of all the thirteen ratnas. Of course, in the last canto, the powerful wheel, or chakri, which gives him and every king the title chakravarti, had already been seen. In this canto we see the arrival of the thirteen ratnas or gems.
2. Bhagyoday means when your bhagya or fate is flowering.
3. See footnote 1.
4. When destiny feels something ought to happen, it happens.
5. Srivats is an auspicious symbol which is often seen on the chest of a Tirthankara. It is one of the eight auspicious symbols or ashtamangalas. The other seven are the Swastika, Nandavarta (a kind of mandala), Vardhamanka (a food vessel), Bhadrasana (a seat), Kalasha (a pot), Darpan (mirror) and Meena Yugala (pair of fish).
6. The ratna called mani is found on the head of the elephant.
7. It is just a way of saying how can one ever remain young, it seems so improbable.
8. Chakri means one who owns the chakr, that is, the emperor Bharata.
9. One yojana is an ancient measure of length/distance.
10. Bharata's army has come to conquer the mountainfolk.
11. Khadag is unparalleled in strength on the battlefield and its target is never missed.

12. Kuldeva refers to the rain deity Meghmukh, to whom the leader of the mountainfolk prayed.
13. Meghmukh is the god of rain.
14. Wind fans fire, so it knows its speed. The bee however flies itself, so how can it measure the speed of wind?
15. The name of the flower used is parijat. This flower blooms at night.
16. This is a comment on how the mountainfolk felt. Power attracts more power, like a magnet. Who will listen to those who have no power?

Canto XI

This canto tells us more about Bharata's conquests. War now breaks out between Bharata and Nami and Vinami (who had been given the kingdoms on the Himalayas by Rishabha). They were the vidyadharas or repositories of knowledge, so they fought equally and the war waged for twelve years. Finally, they were defeated by Bharata. They then bowed to Bharata and apologized for putting up such a resistance. They shower Bharata with gifts and Nami also got his daughter Subadra (name not mentioned in the text below) married to Bharata.

Their conversation indicates that Nami and Vinami are now moving towards renunciation.

In addition to the fourteen ratnas, Bharata is believed to have got nine treasures. The following verses describe them. *Tanam*, section 9, sutra 20–22, describes the different ratnas. As mentioned before, they are all called ratnas because they are the best in the category to which they belong. The nine treasures are: Naisarp, which gives all the knowledge about the construction and planning of village, town, canopies, houses, etc. Panduk gives not only knowledge of mathematics but also how to measure the potency of seeds and grow crops from them. Pingal gives all the knowledge about ornaments for women, men, horses and elephants. Sarvaratna is the source of seven ratnas of single senses and seven of the five senses. Mahapadma teaches everything about garments, their dyeing etc. Kal gives the knowledge of all that happened over the past three years, knowledge of a hundred types of sculpting, and useful lessons for the people like defence, agriculture and finance. Mahakal gives the knowledge of the creation of iron, silver, gold mines, pearls, gems, crystals. Mannavak gives knowledge about arms, ammunitions, shields. Shankh gives knowledge about drama, dance, the four types of poetry and all types of musical instruments.

All the treasures are ruled by divine beings of the same name. They are decorated with inlaid gems and the sun, moon and the wheel are engraved upon them. The rest on eight wheels are eight yojanas long and eight yojanas in width. They are all found on the banks of the Ganga.

Having got these nine treasures, the emperor is now returning home to Ayodhya. Everyone is happy that the king is back. Just as the day and night are the order of the universe, so too are a king's travels to conquer and his absence from town. But now the people look forward to a period of peace and harmony and so they are rejoicing.

Bharata returns to Ayodhya

The ever-favourite dream is made of the desire to conquer the world
But when have we ever been able to own the garment of desire?
Desire opens a world so wide
While necessity requires things so minimal

Even atop the highest peak of the Himalayas
Are two ranges like the jasmine adorning a woman's plait
So too has north and south its own demarcations
And when has darkness ever been close to the sun?[1]

Nami and Vinami, both educated brothers
Because of education they have ocean-like depth
Message from the king the messenger brought
May the earth be the base and shelter be the chakri

I, Adinatha's son, becoming chakri have come
Everyone took the order with humility and respect
In every breath was writ their inherent faith
Every cell of the body full of modesty and humility

After a discussion, the two of them sent a reply
The compassionate Rishabha has always trusted us
We are adopted sons, natural heirs thereby
Only to Adinatha's feet are we indebted

When did you give us the kingdom, Bharata! Look,
to become emperor, do not expand your kingdom beyond limits
You are the elder brother, respect there is for you
The obsession to rule all is an ambition gone too far

You remain on the plains, we inhabit the mountains
Let us see how you win
To everyone his independence is precious
Does the bed of saffron bloom in a forest fire?

The Lord divided his kingdom of his own free will
And on the strength of dedication, the kingdom we took
How can the earnestness of dedication go waste?
The Himalayas will shine with brilliance of education

It will be correct for you to return to Ayodhya
However many rain-filled clouds you may send, they will slip
off this land
If war is what you love, we will not be left behind
Everything we will endure that Gurudeva[2] desires

Armed, Nami and Vinami came along the sky path
Surprise! Unseasonal though it be, the sky was overcast
Will there be a compromise between the earth and the sky?
On every person's face this lone question hovered

Bharata motivated by the chakra to be the world conqueror
Nami and Vinami, leaders of the ascetics and the learned
Both were steadfast in their own stand
Amassing power is a trait that is full of strife

On both sides sounded the drums calling for war
They were armed, nor was there a minute's delay
The learned were intoxicated with their learning
At every step the expectation of victory charged them on

In the chakri army, the chakra lent fearlessness
The divine power also became a defender
Victory was definite to the last penny
The orange flag would definitely fly

Days went by, months went by, even years
Victory and defeat stood unrelenting, shoulder to shoulder
For after all, when has one churned water to get butter?
Or when has the golden lotus descended from the sky?[3]

Loss of humans and material wealth is limitless in battle
And yet the desire to engage in war is an inherent human trait

For twelve years did this clash of power go on
To which star can we attribute this aggression?

The proposal to compromise came from the learned[4]
King Bharata called all his friends and relatives immediately
Waves of relief and joy swept through their faces
Yesterday's enemy was apple of the eye at this moment

O elder brother! You will always remain elder
O great son of Rishabha! Forever great you will remain
But what should be the dharma of the elder?
This only a great person will understand better

Your orders will be respected and unchallenged
But the unmoving Himalaya will have its say
Why do the people of the plains come to the mountains?
Why do they wish to plant their flag here?

Does power mean ruling over others?
Is this what gives a strong mind confidence?
May the slogan be self-control before controlling others
True victory is when everyone's power is respected

Have you now initiated a culture of calling to war?
And do you seek salvation through subjugating others?
Can man ever unravel this mental knot?
The feet that have moved forward, will they ever stop?

We are all sons of that great father, master!
In mind and word follower of the Lord's way
The Lord gave the mantra of victory over self,
Then why have you conquered others?

Bharata

Brother! Everyone has freedom of thought
This uniqueness of man is hidden in his mind
Intellect silent, nervous system developed
The flow of the river of emotions unrestrained

Recognize the root source of human nature
The dominant trait is to control others, you may know
The fortunate ones with power have boundless desire to control
And that naturally keeps falsifying truth

Nami-Vinami

What you have said is true
But Lord, the answer to the question has not yet been answered
That we are driven by our traits is as true as the day
But remember we must that our father is a Jina[5]

We are followers in the path of detachment
In a life of sacrifice we see our worth
Every action should be without remiss, brother
Let not inner desires ever overtake you

Bharata

Filled with goodwill is your logic
True, the Lord has showered compassion on us

This war is the story of cruelty at its heights
This field the playground of cruelty's will

In vain is the story written on the earth and the sky
Few really read the treatise of life
Now I will try to make the language of the soul
May it become the language of life itself

You each rule your kingdom with delight
That which has passed, remove quickly from your mind
We are all followers of Rishabha
To his grace are we indebted

Gifts galore were by Nami presented
Honour and possessions are sources of bondage
Nami then gave his daughter in marriage to Bharata, and together with Vinami seemed to scale the skies to please the king.

From the Himalayas to the western banks of the Ganga came
Bharata, being blessed with the boon of the nine treasures[6]
Fasting for three days tested his divine energy
With the merit of penance, removed were all obstacles

With the Naisarpa, the construction of the village is carried out
Its expertise is the subject of the treatise of the Vastusastra
Panduk helps in mathematics of measurements
And can assess the potency and yield of seeds

Pingal gives ornaments varied
The voice of the sarvaratna explains dharma
Mahapadma teaches the making of clothes
And the sutra for myriad dyes and colours

Kal keeps you abreast of time and helps recall
ancient skills that add charm to sculptors craft.
Mahakal teaches the discipline of metallurgy
Which is the science of making the throne of the king

Received was the mannavak which is eloquent politics
In administration even the rod becomes a slave to it
Manranjan entertains the common people
While the shankh gives expression to dance and muisc

Now whatever gained before looks small, insignificant
The nine treasures were beneficial, everyone accepted
Science is the root of progress, this is an eternal truth
Ignorance lies at the root of decline, everyone agrees

The waves of bliss are rising above a sea of feeling
Who has seen the ocean in the pot?
Quickly paced will be the progress of our nation
Man's fortunes will be bright

Now the destination is the beautiful city of Vinita
Which is now singing the serenade of war
The thought of going back home
Brings infinite joy and excitement

In foreign land one tends to be aggressive
In one's own land one naturally drops all guard
This is the city of Kaushal, ahead lies Ayodhya
Which has never been defeated by enemies

On the way back home, every tree, every step looks familiar
The trees and monkeys atop them look like family!
The chatter of the cuckoos builds some hidden resolve within
And even the crows cawing seem a soulful invitation to one's home

Filled with fragrance was the atmosphere entire
The farmers with their eyes lovingly caressed the king
A mother's love is the greatest limitless compassion on earth
Bharata epitomized compassion but as an emperor he is new

Without the Lord this path seems so deserted
The dust of five elements on the path touches the feet
O Lord! The collection of your energies
Gives warmth to the world like a winter blanket

The songs of praise are charming
Like pitter-patter of raindrops in summer
Beyond the agricultural lands lies the charming city
Like Alkapuri it is as though descended from the heavens

Quickly they travelled and came to Ayodhya
The people stood on the streets, expectation in their eyes
On aeging faces, new life came to dance
The inner river began flowing deep

The journey for victory has come to an end today
The long wait has come to an end today
The long queue of people saw the emperor Bharata
and felt their hearts fill with unstinted joy

Joy was infinite in the inner chambers
The inner being was peaceful, and outside
new thinking now coursed through everyone
As the irrigated lands caused the earth to sprout

How positive was this sight to behold
It charmed everyone's mind
And no one wanted to
recollect the bygones

In the morning the sun spread pure light
At night the light of the moon came to the fore
When the lotus blooms in the pond of the mind
Then intense darkness is unseated

Our kingdom will be unlike any other in this world
The people of Kaushal will have an evolved lifestyle
In every person will be happiness beyond limits
The desire to wield authority far removed

The evening time has sent the message of its presence
The sun which came at dawn has gone
Just as surely as day follows night or movement, rest
So too is the distinction between light and darkness

May radiance be the life-long companion
Only the clear mind has the right to the day
Darkness is receding so the consciousness can glow
So that in times of sleep too mindfulness[7] remains

Everyone is silent, but the source of speech has gained vibrance
Like the pair of eyes that are closed but the vision they behold
enlarging
Such is the difference between the inner and the outer world
Each to its own as the night and day.

Notes

1. The poet is bringing together contrasts to show the wide division between needs and desire. Even if you go to higher realms, there is duality as he shows with the example of the Himalayan ranges. Directions too have their opposites. Just like darkness has never seen proximity to the sun, desire does not see the boundaries of need. This is an exposition of the philosophy of anekanta.
2. Gurudeva refers to Rishabha here.

3. The golden lotus from the sky is an imagery that has been used earlier as the 'sky-flower'. It indicates the impossible. The verse says both the sides were so powerful that neither victory nor defeat could take place. They were well matched. After all, who likes defeat and so when one has the strength, why would one surrender?
4. Here learned refers to the Vidyadaras for Nami and Vinami were repositories of knowledge.
5. Jina literally means one who has conquered (his senses). The enlightened or the one who has attained kaivalya is called a Jina.
6. Bharata is believed to have got nine treasures. The following verses describe them.
7. Mindfulness is used, as in earlier cantos, to indicate alertness and being in the present.

Canto XII

Bharata, after a few conquests and receiving many gifts, comes back to Ayodhya to be crowned emperor. While the coronation is taking place, the people suddenly notice that not even one of his brothers is attending the function. 'Find out why,' Bharata orders, and the message is clear. It may be noted that even though Bharata is waging war and Jain philosophy decries war, he is following the dharma of a king. As a king, he can and should wage wars.

The brothers are clear, however, that either Bharata reviews his message or they take up arms after getting instructions from their father. So ninety-eight of them trudge up the Himalayas to the presence of their father to whom they explain what has happened.

Bhagwan Rishabha hears them and understanding their predicament says that of course there should not be fighting among brothers. At the same time, to give up without struggle is also not right. The realized one offers a third alternative where he says they can choose a kingdom which no one can take away from them, where bliss is enduring and everlasting. He suggests renunciation.

To illustrate the idea, Bhagwan Rishabha tells a story. There was once a man who used to make coal. He would go into the forest, cut wood and burn the logs to make coal. It was midsummer. The sun was scorching the earth and hot winds were blowing. The man went into the forest and began cutting wood. He was carrying a jug of water. By afternoon he was thirsty. He drank some water. Soon the water was finished. In a short while, he was thirsty again. But his jug was empty. His throat became parched and he yearned for a drink. So stopping his work he went and sat down under the shade of a tree. In the cool shade he fell asleep, fatigued and hot.

The thought with which a man goes to sleep, the same thought plays in his subconscious. He dreamt he was very thirsty. He also dreamt that his jug of water was empty. He then went to a well to draw some water. He drank up all the water in the well and yet remained thirsty. Then he went to the lake and drew in all the water from the lake too. Was his thirst quenched? No. He was still thirsty. Then he went to the river and all the waters of the river he gulped down but still his throat remained dry.

He then went to the water body that was bigger, the ocean, and in one mouthful drunk up all the waters of the ocean. Now all the water bodies of the world were empty. But this man's thirst? It was still acute. What should he do? He went into the desert where the well was very deep and the waters very cool. He reached the well but how to withdraw water from so deep below? He had no tools, no vessel with which to draw water. All that he found lying around were blades of grass. He tied a blade of grass to the rope that was hanging above the well and dropped it into the water. Every time he drew up the rope, he squeezed the grass and hoped that the drops of water would quench his thirst.

Would it?

Bhagwan Rishabha then asked his ninety-eight sons, 'The one who was not able to quench his thirst with the waters of the ocean, will he be able to quench it with these drops of water?'

'No, sire,' replied the sons in unison.

Similarly, the teacher is supposed to have advised his sons to give up a small kingdom and enter a much larger one.

Sabujjaha kim na bujjaha sambohi khalu pechch dullaha
Nno hoomvannamiti raiyo, nno sulabham punnaravi jiviyam[1]

It is easy to get material objects, easy to obtain a kingdom, but gaining understanding and wisdom is difficult. Nights are passing by, life is ebbing away. Understand and awake!

The sons understand what their father is trying to say and after establishing their sons on the throne, they come back to their father to be initiated into monkhood.

Addressing ninety-eight sons

The joy-laden cloud began to shower
The garden of life awoke and blossomed
Up leapt the ocean of the heart in every man
And the animals were filled with unalloyed joy

Of what use is it just to celebrate?
Duty is greater than celebration
So thought the minister
To bring back collective memory

Remains now the coronation of the emperor
The position of the chakri is unmatched
Till now king, he will now on be
The emperor of the whole world

Came the announcement in good time
Chakrishwar will be coronated
In the pure gentle mirror of the eye will be
reflected a beauty beyond words

Atmosphere of anticipation

O sleep! Why would you come?
The mind is not even a bit tired
The sun of anticipation has arisen
The mind is happy and hopeful

How will the king's court be decorated?
How will the coronation be?
And on this alone the mind was fixed
No other stray thought could enter

O night! Why would you come?
The sun has risen on the earth
Why are we indebted to the skies?
Let the earth serenade to the sun

Enthusiasm gave every man's mind
Illumination through light divine
Forgetting sleep and fatigue then
The spirit of wakefulness was born

The golden rays of the rising sun
Touched the earth gently
Good people, acting in unison,
Set a noble example

With the eager steps of the people
Every grain of the earth was adorned
With the union of blessing and effort
The book of life was created

The dignified grandeur of the king's court
Big and sparkling as though of crystal made
In no time was it decorated
And on the throne sat the king

Auspicious tone, auspicious recitation
Became the aural messenger
With amazing ease across the blue skies,
A picture of these emotions spread

Endowed with riches was the court
Endowed with riches were the people
Not even one man was hungry
To all is bread vital

Everyone's lotus eyes were bright
All their hearts filled with love
Jealousy could not take birth
He is human who has love

All the officials came and took their seat
Who were in contact with the people
The tradition of introductions came to be
Nowhere was there any disagreement

The emperor was to be crowned
The officialdom was well-versed and well-known
Not even one brother was in the gathering
In spite of having a hundred of them

In that organization of dignity
Why would friends not pitch in?
Question and disappointment came
Together on the people's faces

Silence reigned in the king's court
Wonderstruck eyes and speechless all
Even the talkative fell quiet
Silence is a difficult discipline

How rare is the sutra of dedication
Or did they not get the message?
Truth is unchanging, in the excess of sensory pleasures
remiss is bound to take place

How much beauty there would be in people!
How much joy there would be in their hearts!
How much pride for Rishabha's family!
How much glory to all!

Looks like in the minds of the brothers
Some nervous tensions exist
Even though no one there is to gossip
Nor are there any enemies

Giving instructions, the emperor sent
messengers to the brothers
Only the lamp can tear through
A blanket of pitch black darkness

Introducing themselves as from the chakri
The message they delivered in humility:
If the desire is for the kingdom, the only
path is through service to me

If the mind is unwilling of service
Then the battleground is the only way
Why should the crown desire thorns?
Service is the beautiful flower of high[2]

Of one thought, one mind, the brothers
gave their reply unanimously,
With the blessings of our great father
Have we got the wealth of this kingdom

Bharata has not the kingdom given
Then of what meaning is service?
Surely this demand has not come without meaning
Service never goes waste

Taking the waters of so many rivers
The ocean still is not content
On being able to sip a little nectar
The bee has become arrogant

Humbled have been the weak kings
Only the soldier remains strong
Sons of Rishabha, equal to Bharata are we all
To everyone is his country dear

If old age he can arrest
Or revert the cycle of death and disease
If subdue his desires he can
Then will he be our Lord Indra

Each and every man is similar
And life for each is set to limits
Then why should anyone be a servant?
We all eat the same grains to sustain life

If war is unavoidable,
We all are ready to fight
Sons of one father we all are
Bharata's is no birth divine

Presenting ourselves in the father's
audience, orders we will take
This is the tradition of the Ikshvakus
To wear his order as our crown

Saying thus to the royal messengers
Towards the Himalayan mountains they went
Under the influence of the moonlight
Life models itself like the chakor[3]

From a network of different routes
One small pathway stood revealed
Every moment seemed year-long
The interminable wait made even hurry seem slow

Unquenchable thirst and unblinking eyes
Keenly desirous the mental state
The desire to behold instantly
Man is but a desire-filled machine

As the Lord appears to come closer
So much farther though he seems
Far and near are relative truths
The near seems far, not so far, near

As the day dawned, the sun rose
But due to brilliant light remained unseen
Through the unblinking eyes the eight-thousand-metre-high
Himalayas now came into view.

Presenting themselves at his lotus feet
That are tender bud-like and beautiful
Cruelty by others on people weak
Arouses immediate compassion in the Lord

Folding their hands, they all said in unison
You know everything, you All-Knowing
To free the mind of mental knots
Few are capable of doing

O Lord, one who is egalitarian
You gave all a kingdom as per plan
We are all happy, but one problem there is
When is there order and peaceful unity in an empire?

What to tell you of the mental state
Of the elder brother, surprising, ignorant
We don't know why conquering kingdoms
has become his life's only goal

At this place of service and justice
Required is a solution
Service alone to the one and only
That is our firm resolve

Having spread the kingdom of power
And expanded the decorated army
Thinks of himself as the head
But how can life be without stable feet?

Lord, from you the message
we got of giving up all
How deprived is our brother
Who sees only the land around him

Lead us, O compassionate one!
What is the duty of this moment?
Lord, to the right direction point
May we hear something beyond the senses, eternal and new

The kingdom did not descend from heaven
Nor did compassion come as a bequest
They have all come from our father
How to give it up, O our Lord!

O Lord, the floods have now rolled in
Give it restraining banks
Who knows how many in this world
can see, and how many are blind?

Presented we have our mind's anguish
Required is the nest for the bird
Desirous of a reply from the Lord
What solution will you to the community give?

Conflict exists between the sun and moon
The pair of hands spell duality
Caught we are in a quandary
Who will ensure unity?

Forceful desire on both sides
The result of which will be war
Only then will the problem resolve
When everyone wisdom acquires

Why are you not acquiring wisdom
Measure you this moment true
The position of a king is rare, wisdom even rarer
Tell me, are all stones and gems of equal value?

One can gain wisdom
Through the fight between brothers
The solution lies in generosity
Which can become the ideal

What is the difference between left and right?
Both are sides of the same body
One water runs through the flowing stream
That which is separate are their banks

What solution will this fleeting
illusory kingdom give you?
Amazing that people get completely
engrossed and forgetful, with something so small

Will you a kingdom rule that is imperishable?
Enduring, everlasting, always blissful
No one can that kingdom snatch from you
And all such attempts will be in vain

Rose their voice in unison
Give us such a kingdom, Lord!
The dignity of the sons of Rishabha
Will forever be protected, Lord

The thought of a new permanent position
Brought new enthusiasm, new emotions
It is natural that the unknown carries
a mystic whiff and fascination

Sweet, loving, affectionate the Lord's speech
Comparable to cool showers of nectar
Like the new life sprouting in the seedling
is nurtured by wind and water from the well

The scorching heat of the month of Jeth[4]
The sand was sizzling, so was the land
The warm air heated everybody
How will then the mind not burn?

What does the sky care for rain or shine?
This is a matter for logicians
There was a mirage at every step
The sky itself was hot, this was no illusion

To go outside of the house
Which wise man will desire
But to the hungry man
God is visible in his bread

It remained a burning furnace
With the embers in the wild desert
Boiling was the sun from the top
And the heat outside was relentless

Bharat lay down beneath a tree
To get a few minutes of respite
Fatigue is the natural invitation to sleep
And with sleep fatigue released

Saw his alter ego in the dream
Who was in great thirst
Drank up all the water of the well
And yet was feeling greater thirst

Waters of the ponds, the rivers
Even those of the ocean drank
Drunk the sky! And yet is thirsty
Indeed desire wears a garment long

Reaching the land of the desert
Saw a well with little water
Thrust a bundle of grass into it
And wrenching it drank water

The thirst water bodies could not quench
How will it be assuaged?
Surprise however when the desire
to renounce opens up!

In my kingdom,[5] expansive and unworldly,
There is no hint of desire
War and conflict shunned completely
No anguish to enter here

Affection is evened out with balance
Unseen is the duality of joy and sorrow
No cycle of the day and night
Events all independent

Everyone is the knower, everyone the seer
None weak or impoverished
Water available easily
No fish thirsty in the sea

Winter-summer, hunger-thirst
None of them cause any pain
Strong, unwavering resolve acts as the armour
Clear is the mirror of the mind

In this great kingdom even
the unknown becomes a friend
See the irony in this world
How friends become unknown

Over the weak the strong ones
With their strength assert themselves
When does the big fish love
the small one with all its heart?

With the strength of his body and the chakra
Bharata was with strength bestowed
Gaining strength man swaggers
Be he young or be he old

Desirous is the flower but
it withers in just a moment
The prick (of the stem) is a constant of life
And often causes awakening

Of this war between brothers
Generations will sing and tell
Just think for a moment—how will
posterity look the world in the eye?

The end result of war is always
Either compromise or alliance
Hostility does not quench the fire
Water is the counter of fire

Son, in personal quarrels, never are useful
iron weapons and armoury
Sweet, gentle interaction is
most efficient to combat pain

The greatest weapon yet is sacrifice
No questions linger in its wake
Desire is a river of the unattained
Only sacrifice no remainder leaves

Decided we have that fight we won't
Our heads we will not in defeat bow
May the path be lit with harmony
Master, a blessing may we receive so

The history of the Rishabha lineage
would be written with the ink of gold
A history which even in their dreams
no one can ever undo or defame

There is no other way, Lord!
To realize the soul is our only goal
Against the grandeur of the soul
Our kingdom and reign pale away

The soul we will experience
Firm in our decision, a firm resolve
Only complete surrender is
the Kalpavriksha and Chintamani of this age

Lord, how will the throne of the king
remain unoccupied?
We will surrender at your feet
After performing the coronation of our sons

The earth witnessed, the sky witnessed
The conflict between the animate and inanimate
At the end of it all, the garland of victory
Saw the rise of the consciousness.

Notes

1. The first line of the verse has been quoted by Acharya Mahapragya in the canto below. The original occurs in *Suyagado*, vol I, ch. 2:1 as edited by Acharya Mahapragya and published by Jain Vishwa Bharati.
2. Bharata gives them an ultimatum. Either surrender or be ready to fight. As a king he needs to acquire more and more power.
3. This is a beautiful similie. The chakor is also called the chukar partridge. It is in love with the moon. In this context it means that once the moon is up, the chakor can think of little else. Similarly, the ninety-eight sons could also not think of anything else but seeking advice from their father and so they went to him.
4. Jeth is the month between June and July.
5. The kingdom described here and in the following few verses is the one within each one of us—it is the kingdom of the soul.

CANTO XIII

Once again, from the battlefields the scene shifts to the battlefield of the mind. Such quandary is there in life, dictated as it is by the four aspects: matter, consumption, wealth and our reaction to them. While our life's goals and ambitions are governed by the quest for wealth and therefore matter and its consumption, none of us pause to think and reflect on the meaning of life. So we do not act. We only react to our environment and to the people around us. There is therefore never anything new or inspiring in our behaviour.

Bharata's ninety-eight sons search for the soul and look for ways to purify it. They implore their father to teach them how to go about this.

They sit under trees, but that act alone does not bring realization. The verse highlights some of the qualities they need to develop, like detachment. Attachment is the cause of all problems. How to develop detachment? Sorrow, says the poet, is the waste that is produced by dissatisfaction, or not being able to get what you want. Restraint is the key, and to live a life of restraint should be their goal they realize.

While they are thinking thus, in the palace another scene is being enacted. Bharata comes to meet his sister (Bahubali's twin) and finds she is emaciated and as though in penance. Yet, there is a radiance about her. He understands that she wants to become a nun; she wants to renounce everything and join her father's fold. Bharata is all admiration for her and takes her to Rishabha.

Bharata's character is interesting. Even though he conquers and rules with power and pelf, he seems to be an emperor who follows the code of conduct prescribed for a king. As a person too he has spiritual tendencies. He reflects: what am I doing? I am left all alone. He is aware that he is very much a part of the material world and so feels self-conscious about meeting his family who have all become 'nobler' because they are renunciates now. The powerful question here is: who has remained faultless after gaining power?

Rishabha pulls up Bharata by telling him that knowing fully well that he is engrossed in matters of the state, he should not just pretend to understand detachment and renunciation. Bharata listens to him. Yes, he admits, he is in love with his present situation.

Bhagwan Rishabha then tells Bharata a little bit about the future too. He mentions that his son will be born as a Tirthankara many years later. So if there is an emperor fully engrossed in worldly attachments, the same family tree also has a Tirthankara, a completely detached soul. He speaks to Bharata of the only kingdom that cannot be vanquished, the kingdom in which he alone can be the uncontested leader—the kingdom created on the basis of detachment. The son Rishabha is talking about is Marichi. He is Bharata's grandson and is believed to have been born as Mahavira later.

Sundari[1] takes initiation

However dark the clouds be, even if
dyed with the blackness of catechu
They can't forever and forever
cover the sun with their illusions

Matter-consumption-wealth-reaction[2]
This quadrant symbolizes the path to a life of comfort
Illusions are destroying peace such that
we remember not any beginnings or ends

The kingdom of the bud-like mind is amazing
In its flowering one finds the meaning of life
Just as gems were got from churning the ocean[3]
Churning brings even butter to rise

There is butter in milk; boil milk
Set it into curd and churn to get butter
Similarly with penance-prayer and meditation
Realize the beauty of the soul

Saw the city—beautiful it was
Even more beautiful the palaces
The king's feast was enjoyable
So said all the citizens

All that done, to the forest dwelling
they came and with the local people sat
They could not say, nor could they know
Experience is strange, thought the Kiratas[4]

Thoughts by nature are luminous
In their natural state they do not expression find
Through this body and mind made of matter
They find expression in the form of speech

In this physical state of the body
Everything is understood only by articulation
The object and symbol are synonyms, that is why
in varied forms appearances find manifestation

The living and non-living—both
are the basis of material life
To find the soul in it, required
is the culture of initiation

Ninety-eight sons

Lord! I am eager for the moment of awakening
A thousand salutes to awakening!
But from every leaf of the tree in whose shade I sit
is dripping deep and wasteful slumber

The path which carries your footprints
That alone will be our way
The teachings you have reflected upon
That alone will be our guide

Knowledge be that alone, goal be that alone
That alone be the first teacher
The superior truth you have discovered
That alone the abode of the superior soul

Rishabha has brought ever-glowing light
into the landscape of our hearts
For when he initiated his sons into a life of equanimity
They lost the desire for more and more instantly

On the occurrence of these events
Everyone breathed a sigh of relief
That breath alone gave confidence
Which resonated with faith

One ray of the sun does
destroy dense, resolute darkness
One word of the Lord will in life
fill it with never-ending light

What should be the style? What should be the state?
How to sit? How to sleep?
How to eat? How to speak?
How to silence the restless mind?

How to increase mental strength?
How should the strength of forbearance rise?
How to reduce the attraction
towards the body and objects?

Service powered by the desire to know
Elicited the flow of teachings
A drop of water in the oyster under the star of Swati
becomes a pearl, thus portraying the ideal[5]

Restraint in the pace
Sitting and sleeping in restraint
Restrained in the intake of food and drinks
Restraint silences the mind

The strength of detachment
And of giving up, immeasurable
Firm resolve is like the Kalpavriksha
All together build mental strength

With every event experienced together
May there be mental bliss
The feeling of joy can withstand sorrow
Sorrow is but an effluence of hardship

The one who lives in the lap of nature
Knows how to bear the war of joy and sorrow
Keeping the thoughts spotless can
rid the mind of duality

In the whirlpool of the material world
The focus of attraction is the body
The waters are visible, but far away
The banks of the ocean invisible are[6]

To see and establish contact with the soul
The source mantra is that of detachment of
Attachment is what creates the distance
and keeps you in ignorance about the soul

The bright lotus blooming in the sun
Forever turns its face to it
Everyone's mind blossomed
After hearing the Lord's advice

Bharata and Sundari

Limping like a withered bud
she was, in the inner chambers
On seeing her have awakened
Strong stirrings of compassion

Attendant of Sundari

The embodiment of penance is Sundari
Adorned she is with prayer and sacrifice
An incarnation of knowledge and perfection
Amazing spiritual tranquillity in her body

Bharata

Surprising! Some years ago
When body was understood as but matter
The river of life has changed its course
To estimate the new ways is not easy

Eating is an intrinsic trait of man
Then what does fasting signify?
Searching for meanings, especially the
meaning of life, never goes in vain

Attendant of Sundari

The question of daily bread is indeed important
But bigger than that is resolve
in the firm commitment towards initiation
Lord! The bread is but a gross thought

The incomplete progress towards initiation
That has caused this
weakness of the body
Is resolved by the celebration of restraint

Bharata

Worry has turned to contemplation
All this is my doing
No one else is to blame for this
Your servant I am to follow your orders

The impediment to following self-restraint
What should be its atonement?
With money everything cannot be gained
Pure heartedness should be the foremost trait

Initiation is not so easy, forgive me
for saying so, after all to seek forgiveness
is also a holy act, my sister divine
Pure in character as the lotus flower

I begin a journey to the Lord
The reason is the order of Emperor Bharata
In a second was his order followed
And into the samvasaran[7] they made their way

And so the earth turned on its side
And the sky let out a happy cry
Enveloped with its golden aura
The sun shared its enlightening rays

A dream came true when Sundari was initiated
In the presence of the Lord
Initiation is the best way to
practise living in the moment

Introspection by Bharata

Bharata, what kind of life is yours?
Like a tree without its branches
How can anyone separated
from his family be prosperous?

Lord, how will I be able
to meet my friends and family?
Gaining the position of total power
in this world, who has remained faultless?

Desire for kingdoms fills me with shame
Sorrow that I have made such a mistake
How will I find it open my Lord
Closed have I the door to enlightenment

Bowing his head spoke Bharata
Friends, this entire kingdom
Humbly today invites everyone
To enjoy this great big empire

Now is the right time for enjoyment
After which we all will take to ascetism
Let us evaluate on the basis for which time is right
Why do we have so much faith in the imperishable?

Rishabha

Attraction you have to the perishable
Your brothers are engrossed in the imperishable
The kingdom is of great attraction to you
From that all of them are detached

Face it if you wish Bharata
But do not give lip service
Let those who are in matter engrossed
Seek these alms from you

Bharata

Salute to you, Lord
To the world you have given new eyes
May I also see the eternal truth
This will be the greatest blessing

Lord, into this new society
You breathed life anew
Your divine, brilliant aura
Has become the people's support

Mutual support collectively
Sensitivity, compassion, equanimity
In the making of an ideal society
All this must work in conjunction

Expectation there is in the samvasaran
Is there a person who
I can measure against Rishabha?
Whose life is as blessed?

Everyone knows the present
And knows that which is manifest
To describe the future is difficult
Invisible, mysterious is the un-manifest

A small seed gives rise to the banyan
In that is hidden an entire life—
The stem, branches and bough
The trunk in its entirety

Heir yours, named Marichi[8]
A unique script of the future
Who knows in what form
is drawn the line of the best?

As an emperor he will rule over the eight directions
And as the fully empowered divine being be the first ideal example
The last Tirthankara of the greatest religion he will be
So spoke Rishabha words supreme

Of the gushing forth of the emotions
One of them leaped up to touch the sky
Full of joy when man comes
in the proximity of the Great One

Wonderful game this of the subtle world
Even more amazing the subtle waves
The message had reached the gross
And so was heard the sharp tongue of a subtle wave[9]

From outer space is descending today
Bliss without any seeming reason
In the experience of that which is ordained
Each one has his own pace, his own meter

The leaves and flowers become visible
Hidden to the eye is the root
In the eyes that only see flags being hoisted
the flower alone remains visible

In the conscious soul
Natural bliss was born
Seeing King Bharata amongst them
The experience felt very real

Divine being, emperor, Tirthankara—
Rare trio, your son! Your good fortune
At one end it is a full play of passion
At another is total detachment

In our dynasty, in our family,
Who can be valued in this measure?
The sky on earth, the earth
in the sky, all directions silent

I will be the first divine being
First emperor my father
First Tirthankara my grandfather
Ever to arise in the Naabhi lineage

In our family! In our family!
Bliss could not be contained in the heart
Who has measured the extent of bliss
In the lap of the small earth?

Based on physical strength, jati and lineage
The human society is forever tormented
Outside is where conflicts begin
Inside is the kingdom of the ego

Every human has a soul
And all the souls are similar
It is imaginary to compare them
as small or big, important or less so

From the soul came the gentle stream
of lessons in equanimity
How will that be acceptable to the ego?
That will require in-depth research

Who has seen the end of existence?
Who has seen eternal spring?
Turning the endless into the perishable
That indeed makes a sage.

Notes

1. Rishabha's daughter and Bahubali's twin.
2. As opposed to action, it is believed we are only reacting to things and situations, not acting of our own accord.
3. This refers to the well known motif of churning of the ocean in Vedic mythology where, on doing so, a lot of gems were brought forth.
4. Kiratas are tribal people who live on the mountains and have found reference in ancient texts like the Mahabharata and Jain mythology. Even today there is a Kirat tribe on the Himalayas. Scholars are not certain if the two are one and the same.
5. It is believed that when a drop of water falls into the oyster (scientifically speaking it is a substance called nacre) under the star of Swati, it turns into a very beautiful pearl. The English name for Swati is the star Arcturus.
6. This verse is saying that we get lost in this material world thinking only of our body. We know there is more to the body, but that is easily overlooked; we completely forget the existence of our soul. Just as we see the waters of the ocean, but the shore, which is where we have to rest and in this context the soul, being far away, is not visible at all.
7. Samvasaran is the assemblage where the Lord preached in the presence of humans, gods and animals.
8. Rishabha is speaking to Bharata saying your son named Marichi will be a great person. He will be king, Vasudev or a divine being with all qualities and the last Tirthankara Mahavira. It is believed it is Marichi's soul that came to be born as Vardhamana or Mahavira.
9. The prophecy that Marichi would be king, divine being and the last Tirthankara invited a comment from someone in the masses that everything had been kept in the family, and that it seemed like nepotism. The sharp tongue is a reference to that.

Canto XIV

Back in the palace, Bharata is relaxing. There is contentment in his mind. He has won several wars, so he can now concentrate on his spiritual development. But his army chief Sushena comes to tell him that the chakri is not moving into the armoury. Nothing they do is making it move.

'But why should that happen?' asks Bharata in wonder. The army chief tells him that maybe there are yet unconquered territories to be annexed.

'Which one?' wonders Bharata. Sushena is at first reluctant to tell him.

So he cajoles Sushena who ultimately comes out with it. His brother Bahubali's kingdom is yet unconquered. Oh no! Bharata recoils at the idea. Bharata loves Bahubali. And Bahubali is known for his strength. Would it be wise to attack him? Bharata is reluctant to act upon Sushena's advice, and yet as an emperor, how can he not act?

So eventually a messenger is sent to Bahubali with the note: either accept my superiority or come to war.

The messenger goes to Bahubali's kingdom and when he is announced, Bahubali gets excited. He can smell the fragrance of his motherland and news of his brother makes him recount the many incidents between the two when they were children. Once they were inseparable and today they are living so far apart, he reflects.

Bahubali then listens to the messenger. Ours is a relationship between brothers, not between a ruler and subject, declares Bahubali. The messenger plays mischief as all messengers do and Bahubali's patience is teased. Finally, he refuses to accept Bharata's authority and declares that he is ready for war.

Sending of a messenger

On the lotus face of deities[1] of the directions
Played a captivating smile
It was a new journey
of the bouncing rays of delight

The joyous lines of victory
Are spread across the forehead
The sun is rejoicing as it were
The deer is leaping high (as though) to touch the sky

In a second the vision changes
This is the way of the world
Between the clouds and the wind's ways[2]
Some unexpressed love there seems to be

The night follows the day
This is well known
Tell me, who is such a man
Who gets to see only dawn?

On the one hand, the simple folk
are felicitating him
As though bathed in nectar, the mind
is blossoming like a new bud

Peaceful the soldier is standing
His hands folded in humility
Silent speech and a face
expressive of devotion

Bharata

Even after wearing the garland
of victory, O Sushena, you are sad
Every cell of the body is content
Then why is there still thirst in the throat?

Touching you are the heights of success
With the strength of your valour
And yet escape you want to
From the love for victory

Victory and intoxication, both
are words with the same meaning
The message from Rishabha alone
is a measure of peacefulness

The heart is throbbing
With the pride of being an emperor
The restlessness of the monkey
Tells the history of the restive mind

Sushena

From the attachment to victory
Where am I free, O Lord?
Filled with the attachment to victory
Come here I have

On which peak of the Himalayas, Lord,
is anyone still seated on the throne?
How is the compass showing
a state of directionlessness?

Bharata

Today soldier, your
language of emotion is poetry
Then is anywhere, any type
of war still a possibility?

Sushena

Lord, this life of man
is a battlefield in every way
To gain victory in it
Fans our vanity

Bharata

The goddess of war is satisfied
Accepting the sacrifice of many lives
How can this war give man, then
An extension of life?

Desire feed one's own ego
And is the cause of all war
The battlefield drenched in blood
Is angry with the cruelty of man

A war is the obvious rejection
Of the other's existence
A tool for subjugation
It is a destruction of creation

If goodness is what you desire
Of humans, of the world
Arms should just be ornaments
And blessings should be showered upon the armoury

Sushena

Lord, the chakra is the problem
Which is stranded outside the city limits
In spite of enormous efforts
Unmoving it is

It is giving the message that even now
There are enemies left to be conquered
Once again the bugle will call for war
There is still territory to be seized

Bharata

Of victory the sky is witness
And witness is the earth too
The ocean of conflict has been swum across
Every direction has been conquered

Why then is the chakra waiting outside
And not coming into the city?
Why is it not respecting
its position in the armoury?

Minister, find the best way
This is the dharma of the intellect
The secret principle of success
Is good counsel

Which corner remains
Unconquered by victory?
Who is the king who
is still clad in his pride?

Minister

Said the minister, head bowed,
That which is known is inexpressible
Knowledge is such a vast ocean
And inadequate is the world of words

Silence is the best of means
It is the verdict of the wise
Filled with peace, every direction is
And yet thirst is still alive

Bharata

Minister, why are you taking
The side of darkness today?
Why are you not quickly disrobing
The body of ignorance?

Suddenly today, why this vow of silence?
Is speaking such a sin?
This unnecessary restraint on speech
Is that not a curse?

If in times of problems
The chief himself becomes an ascetic
Becoming the flower of Rohitaka[3]
Takes comfort in the promise of fragrance

You are the chief for the son of Rishabha
A position of great dignity[4]
Let your entire being experience
the moon which is resplendent[5]

Minister

Desire I that being artful
I remain ever successful
Silence is my support
Why should I utter words not sweet to hear?

Everyone loves to hear what they like
To speak for pure benefit is only in name
Between two hearts, words spoken unpleasant
Can cause a complete divide

Bharata

Fearless be, I grant you, and truth speak
The earth alone is witness
Be free just as to be airborne is
the intrinsic nature of wings

True it is that bitter medicine is not liked
But does neem not benefit the health?
The rays of the moon in the sky
Are reflected in the waters down below

Truth is what I wish to hear
With an intellect I am endowed
The blessing of the intellect influenced by truth
Is like a never fading flower

Why so much hesitation today?
The real reason is not forthcoming
When the perspective is pure,
Every corner, every grain is beautiful

Minister

Truth I want to tell
But in love I believe
To be the slayer of friendship
Is the curse of bitter words

Conflict between the two eyes
Even as a dream, a thought fearful
With one's own younger siblings
Muscle power is but quagmire

Bharata

Bahubali has not been conquered, minister
Is this not what you wish to say?
To wage a war with one's own kin
Is that not surprising?

In-fighting amongst the sons of Rishabha
Is not what I desire, either
The chakra is displeased, so be it
It is after all not a relative

Minister

Wisdom lies in being discreet
This, my Lord, I have said before
Fast flowing is the rush of waters
Like the banks I've been left behind

On the side of peace I am
But that which is meaningful
The result of one-sided friendship
Is just destruction

When the stream of love flows
from only one side, it is incomplete
The flower without fragrance
And the younger brother an expression of arrogance

In our lands and abroad
This fact is well known today
That greater than Bharata is the
strength of Bahubali

In conquering smaller kingdoms
Why did you your energy waste?
Will the lamp of the seat
of the emperor burn with those conquests?

Of conquering Bahubali, why did you not dream?
You know, the other victories, were merely in name
The true reckoning of your supremacy
Lies in emerging victorious in this battle

The title as the one who has conquered all
Can still not be donned by you
Fulfilment of the above should your resolve be
And then the fragrance of fame will spread about

Delivering a talk that was short and small
The minister fell silent again
Seeing the import of the words, silence reigned
Sound got lost in the skies

Bharata

Logic is strong but
Conflict is only in emotions
If all matters are carried out by words
Then who in this world is rid of discord

Came a change of thought
Man is of strange nature
The relationship between brothers
Is now wobbly and unstable

In Bahubali's humility
To be sure there is doubt
Correct is your insinuation
That amity here is one-sided

The elder one is respected on
earth and the sky
From the young one's conduct
is oozing visible pride

Subjugated are the six regions, emperor,
The brother alone is not humbled
When light is spread in all directions
How is this night surviving amidst it all?

The home is not under control, chaos
reigns everywhere in subjugation
To give only the other the strength
What kind of mantra is this?

That to wage a war against the younger
is problematic, that is true
If the younger one does not obey orders,
Is this also not a problem?

Attachment to either side
Better than that is to be free
Benefit is greater in this world
Affection is, after all, only affection

War is the last recourse, but if
that be given the first place
Then the sweet tree of relationships
How will fragrant flowers bear?

Let the messenger go to Bahubali
with a message from me
If the knot is unravelled
Then let the matter be put to rest

The messenger was fully educated
And initiated skilfully
He was imparted teaching that would
uncover the secret under the guise of affection and love

Gaining wisdom and approval
He is leaving on his way
Unclear being the lines of destiny
The expectation was of victory

War or conflict is resolved
Only as a gift of time
To seek the shelter of silence
Is to respect peace

The life-giving source of passion
Lives for but an instant, short-lived it is
In every moment of calmness, to pause
a second to reflect is an act of spiritual progress

The departure of the messenger

From the retinue of men, the messenger is the
one instructed in rules and articulate
Patient and brave and by name Suveg
He was by employment a spy

Towards the new project at hand
Leaving home and the city of Vinita he left
towards the region of Bahali
As naturally as the tree that bears mangoes

People's talk

Who is this king?
No, not a king, he is a messenger
Why is he being sent by Bharata
Who himself is so attached to Bahubali?

The desire to win over Bahubali
Is now riding high
Ensnared by desire is the elder
The younger free from all of it

Bharata has won over all the kings
Bahubali is happy
When has the depth of the water
been pleased with the shore?

Greed increases with gain
This is an eternal truth
Bharata's endeavours will be
fruitless, this is certain

Hearing these bitter conversations of the people
The messenger is upset at heart
Concerning their own king
Why are the people not accepting?

Is it fair here to sing
the praise of Bahubali?
Why is the thinking that Bharata
is just a star, and Bahubali the sun?

Even though lost in deep thought
The messenger moved forward rapidly
The first sign of movement and progress
Is the end of immobility

The sweet twitter of birds
And inhaling fragrant air
Welcomed by charming lotuses
He entered the land of Bahali

Farmers, each on their lands,
Engrossed in their threshing ground
The siddha yogi is immersed
In meaningful meditation

Singing the praise of Bahubali
Are they with great devotion
Their internalized devotion
is blossoming as their strength

An environment of success, filled with
dedication and respect
Just as a beautiful, radiant night
is but a gift of the moon

Tied to the stalk, the bud
blooms into a full-blossomed flower
The natural experience of oneness
is a mutual sharing of love

Hearing the queries of the messenger
The people of the villages said,
The brilliance of Bahubali is incomparable
That of the sun is left far behind

Emanating light alone he is
Free from scorching heat
This land is a gift of the moon
Filled it is with moonlight

Lord one, his subjects we all
Each of us has our land
The clouds showers on all of us
And the efforts of the people are rewarded

The body healthy, the mind is happy
It is a healthy relationship
The burden on us is light and we
have the support of our strong shoulders

In Bahubali's land of Bahali
Unity amongst people and their king
Each person is confident of ownership
In every pair of eyes there is vitality

With the coming of the messenger
Afraid the town of Takshashila is not
The new morn stood alone and strong
In the period of rising fearlessness

The chariot stopped at the doorway
The message the doorman took within
A messenger has come and in
wait his peace has been conquered

The dam of patience, my Lord
Seems to be breaking down
May I meet without delay?
He has asked in a voice soft

Bahubali

From where has the messenger come?
And why has he come here?
Full details I desire
And now where is he?

Sentinel

Coming he is from the motherland
From the beautiful city of Vinita
To deliver the message
From Bharata in good time

Beside the door, Your Majesty
He is waiting
Even though the fish lives in deep waters
It appears thirsty today[6]

Looks like there is excitement
in his heart, and his energy is great
But peeping from within is a sadness too
That makes for a portrait unseen

Bahubali

Bring him quickly, in the
name of motherland there is sweetness

In the grains of that pure earth
Love is abundant

So the messenger was presented
Bowed head and folded hands
Impressed by the brilliance of the king
Was his mind; in spirit he was combat ready

Messenger! Come you have from Ayodhya
Tell me what the matter is
And the land of Bahali
did not repeatedly greet and welcome you?

Then you would have seen for yourself
The oneness of the two brothers
Spread across is the peaceful aura
Even at night as though day

Hope all is well in your country of Kaushala
And the people are all content
Is brother Bharata happy too
With the success of his march to victory?

Delighted is my mind today
Goose pimples I have on my body
All that was sleeping on the bed of memory
Is now completely awakened

In the memories of those days, alone
is there the sweetness of nectar
In the experience of that sweetness
I am today rejoicing

His lap was like the bed itself
A gift of our father it was
I would sit on his lap first
And Bharata would be jealous of that

And when Bharata would be seated
On the lap of our father
I would make him get down
In the typical playful manner of a child

Don't behave impertinently
Bharata is elder to you
Saying this, our father would stop me
His words full of propriety

Once mounted on an elephant
Bharata was engrossed in play
His eyes were scanning the skies above
And seated in arrogance was he

Pedestrian me, I was
to him unnoticed, unseen
The message of courage
I was reading to myself in silence

Taking his feet in my hands
I tossed Bharata up in the sky
Love called involuntarily
In the corner of the heart

Woe! Is this the right behaviour
Towards the elder brother?
Is this befitting the
greatness of Bahubali?

My love for him caused me to
throw open both my hands as though
Getting ready to catch and unblinking
I watched him, born was a moment anew

As children we constantly play
Throwing and catching the ball
Like that I caught Bharata in my arms
Due to overwhelming affection in my heart

Is the enjoyment of the sugar cane
Only for one person?
Why with the younger brother
Is there no sharing of love?

Grab I did aggressively from Bharata
The juicy sugar cane
Silent was the brother
Whatever was there to say, the flow of tears did

Father breaking it into two halves
Gave both of us one part
In duality, oneness, we
then experienced

The story of childhood games
is equivalent to sweetest honey
Of those days and of those moments
Memory is indelible and invaluable

That Ayodhya which breathes
Peace in its every breath
That holy figure of Rishabha
Is eloquent of faith

Along with it comes the memory
Of the hundred brothers too
With the happy events of the time
Excited is my heart

Your coming has invited those past moments
To appear before my eyes
As though to make me believe
That in this room is Rishabha himself

By giving me the kingdom of Bahali
My father has sent me far away
But memory has today
Filled every part of my being

Why has Bharata sent you here?
What is the new message?
How is the wind blowing?
What is the new excitement?

To measure the speed of the
fast-paced horse is easy, very easy
But the speed of the mind is greater
And more restless than wind itself

Messenger

Bharata has marched to victory
Lord, this is well known
Victory is being celebrated
This may be unknown to the brothers

If they knew then far from Bharata
No one would remain
What, would they not reach Vinita
And say two words sweet to him?

Getting the invitation from the messengers
Depressed in mind they were
All the brothers in the Lord's presence
Were initiated as monks

You alone remain
Do think deeply
Leaving your former life
Take to a new way of life

Our kin alone becomes the problem
This is the cream of the teachings of law
Law is such a maverick that
It finds victory even in loss

Do not tune the chord too tight
Recognize reality
Speaking I am as one of your people
Listen you to my advice

The duty of the younger to the elder
Is to be subservient
Woe! In the show of immodesty
You are like a deluded priest

The king is bound by law
And not to his family
In the crown a gentle flower he wears
While in the hand a sword he bears

This advice of the king, Your majesty!
Is in accordance with law and very clear
I accept that to hear that clarity
Causes a pain that is difficult to express

Like the head that bears the crown
May you bear the rule of Bharata
That is the essence, which in brevity
Says everything that is to say

The one whom Indra is giving
Half his kingdom with respect
Its value every man can make
An estimate of by just guessing

My question is, when did the brothers
Take time to estimate this?
The respect owed to an emperor
When did they really give?

The veil over the king's greatness
Is his very family
The love for one's brothers and sons is like
the sword's edge smeared with sweet nectar

An emperor is an emperor
A king is after all only a king
The ocean has its own vastness
The well is after all only a well

The emperor has patience
And that is why he is tolerating you
The weak person will not be able to bear
The heat of the raging fire

Lord! Seek do I your pardon
If I may have uttered some things harsh
If in the discipline of humility
I have remained very far behind

All knowing Lord! The duty
of the messenger is to be beneficial
Words which are seeped in truth
Can only create true benefit

Bahubali

Messenger! Your fine articulation
is praiseworthy
The arrogance of the elder brother
Has indeed a flavour distinct

He thought of the younger brother
At the time of his celebration of victory
In the moments of the march to victory
Did affection hide in fear?

If in the elder there is maturity
Humility is praiseworthy
If the elder lacks the quality of nobility
Humility will inimical be

Flower this, separated from the bee
Is bound to the stalk
But in the power of the bee's hum
Engrossed it is in the attraction

From the grandfather we have learnt
The lesson of self-preservation
And with recollection rises
the lesson from his veritable actions

The feet are moving forward on the path
Messenger, how do I make them stop?
Law modified! How can the head
bow to injustice?

The order established by father is
completely acceptable to us
From the waters of the flow
Grains are nurtured and nourished

Under the heat of the raging fire
Do the crops ever manage to grow?
Even the calatropis tree burns down
In an instant with the force of snow

The art to assuage
the aggression of Bharata
I know, I also agree that
Bharata is beneficial to me

The measure of nobility
Lies in the cessation of war
War is, after all, a fallout
Of ego and pride.

Notes

1. Digvadhus is the word used and they mean the consorts of the deities of direction. For any fruit to be realized the blessing of the Digpala is necessary, and it is always through the digvadhus that it is obtained.
2. For the cloud floats away with the wind.
3. The botanical name of Rohitaka is Tecomella undulate and it belongs to the family Bignoniacea. Two varieties of Rohitaka are found: rakta (red flowered) and shweta (white flowered). Rohitaka grows in Rajasthan, Punjab, Gujarat and in the Himalayas up to 1,000-metre elevation. It has no fragrance.
4. The word used here is solah (sixteen) kala (characteristics). The first five 'kalas' are present in every human being and they are Annamaya (with cereals), Pranamaya (with breath), Manomaya (with mind), Vigyanamaya (with knowledge) and Anandamaya (with joy). The others are Atishayini, Viparinabhimi and Sankramini. The rest of the eight 'kalas' are Prabhvi, Kunthini, Vikasini, Maryadini, Sanhaladini, Ahladini, Paripurna and Swarupavasthit.
5. The verse assures the minister that he is fully trusted and blessed by the king.
6. Indicating that the messenger has come from a prosperous land but his intentions seem like he wants our land too—he is still thirsty for more like fish from deep waters.

Canto XV

The messenger returns to Ayodhya and tells King Bharata that King Bahubali is ready for war. He omits telling Bharata details of how Bahubali remembered him fondly and how he was shocked at Bharata's invitation to war. Bharata is a little disturbed. 'Have I been hasty?' he wonders. 'My brother is so much stronger. Is brotherly love more important, or the duties of a king?'

The general of the army assures him that he is bound by the duty of a king. But Bharata is still apprehensive.

The bugle sounds and both the brothers with their armies stand face to face on the battleground. The first war of ancient times begins and establishes one truth: man's attachment to his ego and power is far greater than brotherly love or any other human relationship. If on one side the desire for power had made one brother attack, on the other side that same desire turned the other brother into an enemy.

Between the brothers four types of combats are announced. The first is drishtiyudh in which the opponents are supposed to keep looking at each other and the one who blinks first loses. Bharata loses this round.

The second is shabdyudh or war with verbal sounds. Here, the one who roars louder is the winner. While Bharata roars loudly enough, once Bahubali begins his voice is drowned.

Meeting on the battlefield

Bharata

You've been a long time, messenger! Tell me,
What message have you brought from my brother?
Was the travel through Takshashila comfortable?
What is the degree of prosperity in Bahali?

Tell me about the mind of the energetic king of Bahali
Is his rasa of pride greater than all the navarasas?[1]
Will the sunflower now fall in line with the sun?
Will the lotus bloom?

Have any notes in the blue-throated peacock's call changed?
Or has darkness set out on a voyage to see daylight?
This seems to be some new tale of a supportive draught of wind
But, remember, no one can rule this world as per his whims

Suveg

O warrior! Your words full of rasa
To hear is my mind ever desirous
As long as your protective hand is on us
We are blessed to be around the emperor

Lord! Some new sights of this journey
Like those never seen and picture pretty
Even now my ears are resounding with the speech
And the echoes of the courageous people of Bahali

They are all dedicated to their king
Like brilliant stars are their warriors of the sky
O Lord, the land of Ayodhya is to us beloved
Bahali rests on the beautiful shore of the river

The people are alert and dedicated to hard work
Embodiments of the love for independence
The scales of independent thinking are heavy with
men and women irritated at the thought of dependence

As the ruler, so the people
From one lamp to another light is spread
Just as pearl glistens through pure water
Every child is radiating the self-pride he has imbibed

The message is clear, the younger brother will not come
From his arrogance he cannot himself separate
One alternative remains between you two,
Egos have combined to ensure war

Both the brothers are plagued by doubt
Generally fights are born of suspicion
Dedication bound together every atom of the Himalayas
Suspicion broke into smithereens every atom of the mind

Introspection by Bharata

Have I taken the right step after right thought?
Or have I stepped forward unheedingly?
In the skies thinking lives, and on earth
The impulsive man deceives himself

Is it right that messenger to the younger brother I sent?
I don't know why the heart has turned to stone?
If love for the younger one had flowed through me
Then it would water the tradition of humility

I forgot the incomparable and excessive strength of the younger
Woe to the haze of forgetfulness! Such is the nature of man!
Huge is the body of the elephant, but petrified is he of the lion
I think I measured my brother's strength rather hastily

Boxing my brother on his back, I turned to run[2]
When as reaction my brother turned my way
Then flashed across the skies the lightning of anger
Drops of fiery energy scattered around smouldering

Cold flow of water on that great fire
By pouring, the Lord, my father, his blessings on me bestowed
Who is greater in courage than Bahubali?
What is this new chapter between brothers?

Who does not the strength of Bahubali know?
In his state of wrath who will now the protector be?
Experienced truth how can I falsify?
How can I tell everyone that which is on my mind?

How to get freedom from this state of confusion?
How will the flower of amity and brotherhood now bloom?
What can be wrought of worry? If he had only reflected a little,
my brother, would he not have come running to embrace me?

The mountain, ocean of river may stand in-between
But tell-tale mischief should not the bond of brotherhood break
The question is significant: Is the emperor bigger, or a brother?
The greatest lesson in the story of brotherhood

And so the self-expression stunned everybody
Is this song sung by the king, sweet to the ears?
The discord between the notes and the tune is evident
What kind of surprising way of thinking the master has!

Everyone was silent but silent was not the mind
In inner expression there is the same pleasure as in talking
Then the chief of army gathered unparalleled courage
Courage alone is the golden crucible of life

Sushena

Lord! Brother he is and brave for sure
Love is the great intellect of weakness sheer
Does politics accept brotherly love?
Kingdom first, relationships are allowed only after

Son of Rishabha he is and brother of Bharata
The greatness of his courage has influenced every human
Who can bear the heat of the army of the emperor?
This emperor can fight even Lord Indra

Those people who at the edge of the kingdom dwelt
With whom the divine themselves dwelt
Were they able to stand before the army of the Lord?
Coming down from the height of arrogance at your feet they fell[3]

Lord, the one truth that is before all of us
This time the wind of victory is blowing
If one remains unconquered, victory is equal to none
In every one is the force of self-sacrifice

What is required is just one sign to raise the army
Hope this heartfelt prayer reaches your inner being
We are confident of victory, Lord! Hundred per cent
Just as the planets naturally bow to the sun

The inner conflict of Bharata

The conflict will be between the sun and the moon
What will happen to the planets and the stars?
Will the beauty of the sky continue to remain unalloyed?
The light of weapons will become an ornament

This family of Rishabha is great and famous
It is proud of its sacrifice and penance
This family has taught the lessons of brotherhood
And taught the auspicious mantra of amity

The family has given pride to the human race
To people in darkness it has shown the path of light
Will it then today invite darkness?
Will the pot of nectar be adulterated with poison?

I do not wish to meet my brother now in war
The teachings of his Lord are in every cell of mine
All the officials heady with power
To them, even more than home the battlefield is loved

This conflicting thinking tells me to keep quiet
That I show forbearance in likeable and dislikeable matters
The message that is expressed by the language of silence
Who has searched for its meaning in words?

In less than a second, the frightening bugle call for war sounded
And instantly with no delay the army collected
Rose the thought that this will be the march to the greatest victory
Long sounded the call in all directions

The limits of Bahali are now within sight
Like a student in learning is engrossed
The lonesome moon is strength on this beautiful earth
Even in this restless event, patience is undeterred

The king of Bahali has received a message from the spy
Danger to our homes comes from within our homes itself
Now the battleground is the only way out
What kind of conspiracy has this wheel of fate carved out?

The soldiers asked of the war-sounding bugle,
Is the battleground to measure our sacrifice today?
The strong one is silent, the prowess of whose arm is weak?
All strength is offered at the feet of the Lord of Bahali

Weave the pros and cons of resolves and possibilities
Aggressive is Bharata, everyone now knows
Has he kept the belief that the elder is wiser?
Who has ever tasted the waters of a mirage?[4]

Bharata should be knowing that his brother's strength is unmatched
Then how did he wear this robe of bravado?
Where is the glowworm, where is the sun—what to say?
How to open the door to the inner mind?

The confidence of victory quickened the pace
The waves of the mind gave birth to the intellect
Reached the limits the flow of anticipation
The fate of Bahali should shine bright

Behind them all were the two brothers
Their armies came to the battlefield
To find pleasure in fighting is an innate trait of the mind
The cuckoo to the crow, the crow nurtures the cuckoo[5]

Man is the beautiful being of the universe
From the sight of his form were words born
Science tells the eternal story of nature
Inside fire and on top of it all water[6]

Only that human is beautiful who glows with amity
What beauty is it if feared by everyone?
All war begins in the mind of man
The battleground is but its shadow or consequence

If Bharata had not sown the seed of war in his mind
Then why would we the King of Bahali on battleground find?
Now preparations are getting set for harvest
Each one has his unique way of working in this world

When one brother is thirsty for the other's blood
Then what hope of amity from soldiers?
Man finds happiness in hurting another
When humanity is hurt, the earth cries

The beginning of verbal war

First war is fought with words
Then threats of weapons dictate it
There is an exchange of hurtful words
Which tear through the chest sharper than an arrow

What cowards are the soldiers of King Bharata?
Is it possible to row a boat of stone?
Why as a piece of rock are you standing on the warpath?
Why do you in vain clash with the army of Bahali?

Will victory over the weak claim glory?
Will the dark, moonless night conquer darkness?
Come into the battlefield, powerful as the sun
Are you thinking of it as your courtyard at home?

Verbal altercations began and physical rage increased
The afternoon sun was right above the head
Now the strength of the body is on the anvil
Who will hold the reigns of war?

The beginnings of weapons came as a form of art
Mental fears turned it around chameleon-like
Muscle power more energetic than punishment
And the one who commanded more men became more powerful

Unarmed combat is the art of Sinhanad[7]
Just like a beautiful woman makes even weapons tremble
With cosmic energy the strength of the mind is awakened
That alone is the gain in this conflict

The emperor called a meeting of the soldiers
And narrated to them the monstrocities of war:
Do not look for the present in the past, he said
Measure the present against today

Be serious, this is not war ordinary
See your faces, this is a mirror
The strong Bahubali's courage is overwhelming
Even courage fears to come too close

Make the right use of the power of faith
Bring with you the fame of being the best army
The cloud gained from supporting winds
To that we owe our victory so far

Bahubali

This is the first time we are faced with war
Brother the attacker, delusion of this world
Waging war is not our goal
To safeguard existence has been the motto

Sacred and determined is our resolve
Will the sun fear pitch darkness ever?
Faith is seating itself in every breath
With the power of caution, the mind and body is filled.

Notes

1. There are nine dominant emotions, as mentioned in Sanskrit literature, which govern human life. The emotions are given in a footnote in Canto V.
2. In this verse and a few ones later, Bharata recollects his childhood interactions with Bahubali.
3. The reference is to the battle with Nami and Vinami that has been described before.
4. The idea here is that there is always a discrepancy between belief and reality: the elder brother is said to be wiser, but is he so in reality? The answer is given with the example of the waters of a mirage.
5. The cuckoo lays its eggs in the crow's nest. The crow look after the eggs till they hatch.
6. Refers to the nature of the earth. It gets more and more hot inside as you move towards the centre, but on the surface there is water.
7. Sinhanad is a form of war where a loud roar is let out to cause fear and destruction.

Canto XVI

The war is on in full swing. The army of Emperor Bharata is a little more aggressive, perhaps, because they are worried. When Bahubali sees their pace and mood, he gets angry and is just about to enter the battlefield when his son Simharath says that he will go first. Let the fathers join the battle later, he requests.

As mentioned earlier, the simhanad is sounded. On hearing Bahubali's roar, the emperor's army makes a hasty retreat. Fear has chilled their bones. Then Sushena motivates them to go back to war and aggressively so.

Sushena's motivation does not last too long as once again the frightened army withdraws. Then Sushena asks Bharata why his son Suryayasha is not leading them. Is he too fond of his uncle? Have emotions entered the battlefield? Suryayasha is provoked and he comes to fight Bahubali's sons Sugati and Mitaketu. They are both killed and Bharata's army rejoices.

'Do not rejoice too soon,' warns Bahubali and prepares to come to war himself. But there is ambiguity in his mind.

Suryayasha says he is there to fight and learn from his uncle. But he asks why should so many soldiers die in a feud that is personal? Here the army ponders—will someone see the futility of the war, they wonder.

Description of the war between Bharata and Bahubali

The seed can and does become a tree
when it germinates
It takes on a form magnificent
When there occurs a tear on its skin

The verbal arrow, more than the one of iron
Penetrates deeper, amazing it is
Different from that of an ordinary meeting
Is the dharma of the battlefield

In the army of the emperor
Was born excessive anger
And so it attacked aggressively
The army of Bahubali

And they fled as fast as the wind
The king of Bahali saw it all
Raised eyebrows wrinkled worry
Anger turned the eyes red

To walk into the battlefield
Bahubali in a hurry began to leave
Said his son Simharath in all humility
The is the arrogance of the ant before an elephant

Sons present and yet fathers fight
What kind of conduct is this?
Everyone agreed that Bharata's army
They will quickly disarm

Moved the chariot of Simharath
And so did their excessive determination
In the flickering lamp, drop by drop
New oil surged in

Trembling at the Simhanad
Was the army of Bharata
Warriors fled from the battlefield
Who was that? Bahubali or Indra himself?

Seeing the depressing situation
The great army chief Sushena
Came forward and awoke
The sleeping pride of the chakri soldiers

On the war ground, victory and defeat
Are enacted with unblinking eyes
And into the army of Bahubali
The army chief entered direct

Today we have gained for the first time
A novel measure of thought
Even outside the land of Bahali
One can find examples of courage and bravery

Only to the army of Bahali
Was granted the boon of victory
So believing, no one ever challenged, for they
reconciled to live as inferior to the people of Bahali

Vidyadhar[1] Anilveg
Took control of the lost forces
The deserting army was called to stop
And Anilveg called for an exhibition of strength

Beside the power of knowledge, muscle power
loses its very meaning
And the army of chakri thought
Now to fight is in vain

His fast-paced progress was arrested in a trice
Like a sudden snowfall
And mentally to Bahubali
The chakri army did salute

Anilveg told the army chief,
In Bharata's army you are brave
But you have not seen the
ocean's other shore

We do not know in the mixture of milk and water[2]
How much of it is water alone
It would be of great help if we could say
This much is water and that is milk

From victory in many wars
Is born this disease of arrogance lethal
There is no cure for this in the world
Except through the strength of knowledge

Weak people you have conquered
Is this victory, O general!
You have not used your muscle strength
Just waved your hands about in empty space

Now keep quiet, Anilveg
In vain do you lament
In the river of vetarani[3]
How will sin be washed away?

What do you know of the strength of the king
And the power of the chakra unlimited?
What do you know of the flower's fragrance[4]
On the land of Bahali there is only neem

Neem is best known for its bitter taste
Rest of its qualities are hidden
You undoubtedly have presented
before me a community of cowards

In this great war of words
Their rage broke free again
With the outburst of verbal power
A new message was being sent

Their knowledge power and muscle power
Was unknown to the earth and sky
In the world of the known and unknown
A new resolve was taking shape

In a second on the earth, next second in the sky
One second in the chariot, the next in a whirl
Taking on an omniscient form they fought
Their foreheads dripping with sweat

In a trice Anilveg broke
The chief of army's bow
Intoxication is like an elephant, mad,
It can destroy an entire dynasty

In the loss that took a minute
The army chief stood aghast, surprised
All his resolve turned into worry
Limp was his mind

All that remained was anguish painful
In hand was the weapon god-given
For Anilveg, definitely, it was his
powerful army that was the blessing

Becoming an obstruction Simharath crossed the path
It arrested the army's speed
Anilveg got security
Agitation and anger spread across everyone

So fierce was the battle between the two
Even the sun could not bear to watch
Going to the lap of the setting west
Was written a new script of fate

The discipline of war
Gave rest to the soldiers
Distancing the enemies when darkness fell
Came they all to their abodes

The sun rose in the lap of the east
In splendour spread its light
To the warriors of old times
Night was a period of repose

O light! You are greatly loved
For the benefit you give to all
In the playground of change
All games are subjective

Undesired the sun rose
Bringing light to reluctant eyes
Weary limbs
Complained in exhaustion

Simharath welcomed the army chief
Taking Sinhakarna along with him he said
Come, army chief, come, these hands
have been waiting long and eagerly to embrace you

Ornamented with divine weapons
The chief of army came forth
With the sound of a lion's roar
Made the soldiers of Bahubali tremble

Again the moment of escape came
Simharath was the cause of such fear
Simhakarna, with his skill and expertise
Now attacked the army chief Sushena

The sun is becoming witness to see which soldier
will be the favoured recipient of victory
Victory herself is a collection of doubts
Whose body is as strong as steel?

Opportunity has its own strength
Sometimes power may be in one hand
Sometimes in another's
So the many turns of the wheel of fate

Depressed and wounded
The chariot of the army chief returned
It was as if the sun had departed
Untimely to its abode in the west

Anilveg saw an opportunity
And taking the speed of wind
Landed in the army of the emperor
Causing an uproar like a rising wave in the sea

The elephant-mounted emperor saw
The courageous play of Anilveg
He saw his army desert the ground
And he saw him laugh at them

Burning with anger Bharata
Threw the divine powerful chakra
With the flames seen in outer space
Wonderstruck were the celestials—Indra and all

Behind Anilveg it sprung
Like a leopard on its prey pigeon
In the power of the chakra
The army of Bharata's land had great pride

With the power of knowledge Anilveg constructed
A security shield so strong
And then like a bird in a cage
Becoming fearless took respite[5]

Thereafter from the unequalled power of the chakra
Anilveg was not able to protect himself
Without any penance, by itself
The body fell away, motionless

Vidyadhar Ratnari[6] with anger
Was burning as he saw the sight
With the speed of wind he came
As though he could end the war

With skill and expertise he twirled his mace
As though to churn the enemy army with[7]
He massacred them one by one
And left no sign of life thereafter

On the strength of the king of Bahali
Unparalleled hope of victory rose
In the war field to kill
the enemy becomes the desire, of course

The criminal who kills
Is celebrated as the greatest
And the man whose chest bears
countless wounds of war is called a hero

The army chief Sushena saw
the aggressive attack on his army
The desire to desert the war ground, he thought,
becomes a gift to the losing side

Like the sky overcast with black clouds
Sushena, the army chief, came to Bharata
Blurting out his inner anguish
Said, 'Lord! They are laughing at us.'

The army of the king of Bahali
Is rich in strong soldiers
And our army, O Lord
Is like fish out of water

Master, your son is as strong as you are
And yet the massacre of the army we see
Surprising it is on the war ground
Familial bonds that are weakening

Is he hesitating because of such bonds?
Or else, what would be the cause of such cowardice?
Winning is the smaller army
Losing is the army of greater numbers

Silence as intense as an ocean of peace
The king was in the stance of deep thought
The words pierced his heart like an arrow
Spoke the invincible Suryayasha[8]

The sun will be witness in this war
of new aggression, with the new sun
all the stars will hide themselves
Only the younger brother will remain

Delighted was the army chief to hear
Successful was this last shot of his
Night took leave immediately
Spread the unending light of the sun

Suryayasha with the brave brother Shardul
Came to see the war front
Sugati and Mitaketu[9] were engaged in
the torture of Bharata's army

Stopping the chariot of Suryayasha
Vidyadhar hero Mitaketu
became the bridge, you grandsons of Rishabha
Mitaketu does not trouble without reason

Shardul was stopped by Sugati
The sun was witness to the flying of many arrows
As though on the empty skies was splashed
a loud and angry accusation

Shardul was caught in the net of Sugati's
Tight grip as though that of a snake
Freed he was with Garuda's[10] expertise
And again rose in war with cyclonic speed

Leapt as though a leopard on a prey bird
Tore open Sugati's head
In the annals of the cycle of time
How many secrets are hidden?

In the dictionary of the treatise on war
There is a total lack of verses on compassion
That much fame as much as the number
of deep wounds on the enemy's chest

Sorrowful was Bahali's army
Joy tumbled forth on Bharata's side
Woe! Woe! Destruction of one
Becomes the joy of the other

Indignant King Mitaketu
Attacked Suryayasha
More and more aggressively
In reaction to the death of Sugati

The great valour of Suryayasha
Was being combated by Mitaketu
In the playground as though the clever
player is playing faultlessly

The proud head bowed in a second
As though bowing at the feet of destiny
Man becomes true and untrue, for
the game of war is mysterious

The king of Bahali from the back
Saw all that was going on
Who will now be the chief
of the powerful army of Bahali?

This sky bereft of the sun and the moon
How will it be prosperous again?
Without the two vidyadhars, the army
is today seeking shelter

Bahubali himself came to the front
And roared like a lion
Trembling was the emperor's army
Desertion from war ground got a new definition

Bahubali

Suryayasha, you are courageous
The first grandson of the Rishabha lineage
Love is in one corner of my heart
Tarry not here, go search out your family

My brother elder is thinking
My army is an empty forest
But in the cave is the lion,[11] a heavy
fee will have to be paid

Love is rising in the eyes
On the hands is the blood of affection
Unfortunately weapons are holding the link between us
Disappear of your own accord

Suryayasha

From the great one has come streaming down
The nectar of love divine
But today to fight these arms
two are eager, O one equal to my father

The young elephant walks along the footprints
of the leader of the herd, my Lord
We will learn the expertise of war
For only when you go through fire do you mature

If the waters of compassion of the great ocean
Were equivalent to milk
Then why in these cruel times would
the hand hold the arrow that can kill?

Uncle, all these poor soldiers
deserve sympathy
We always remain secure and safe
But not the soldiers in the forefront

Desirous of humility, revered father
Riding the steed of arrogance
Everyone faultless and for no reason
Suffer the heat of war

Thinking I am that the army
of both sides take rest today
Father, let this ground of war
Become a meeting ground

The heat of the war ground gave way
to the cool showers of compassion
Suryayasha, you are a blessing
A keeper of Rishabha's line.

Notes

1. Vidyadharpati is an adjective often used to mean one endowed with education or erudition.
2. Anilveg is saying his side is made of milk and on his side the supportive wind of victory is blowing.
3. River Vetarini is mentioned in the Samyukta Nikkaya where it is called Yama's river.
4. The flower here is parijat.
5. Anilveg built a cage-like structure to protect himself from the onslaught of arrows. Here he takes some respite.
6. Another soldier on Bahubali's side.
7. The poet is likening the mace to the act of churning. The receptacle is the army and the mace is the churn.
8. Suryayasha is Bharata's son.
9. Sugati and Mitaketu are grandsons of Rishabha and sons of Bahubali.
10. Garuda is the eagle and eagles are supposed to prey on snakes. So the cure for snake bites or anything to do with the snake is also called the art of Garuda.
11. Bahubali is saying that even though his two prime fighters and sons are no more, he is still there, the lion among men.

Canto XVII

At that time an oracle is heard which says: why are you brothers, sons of the same father, fighting? When the brothers say they would not stop fighting, the celestial voice then asks why should the armies of the two brothers fight? Why not the fight be restricted to the brothers alone? This the brothers accept and the soldiers are told to stop fighting.

But Bharata's soldiers are worried. Bahubali is strong, but our master is more gentle, they think. How will he fight? Seeing their despondency, Bharata decides to show them his strength. He makes them dig a deep trench. Then he asks them to tie a thick chain around his arm and then he jumps into the trench. He then tells the soldiers to pull him out of the trench by pulling the chain. The whole army tries, but cannot move Bharata by an inch. Then when Bharata lifts his arm and puts his hands on his chest, the action makes the soldiers fall down, one behind the other.

Between the brothers four types of combats arere announced: Drishtiyudh, Shabdyudh, Mushtiyudh, and Dandyudh. Bharata loses the first two rounds as mentioned in the previous canto.

Mushtiyudh is use of the fist. Bharata hits Bahubali very badly, but when Bahubali retaliates, Bharata falls unconscious to the ground and is defeated for the third time.

Now comes Dandyudh. Bharata wields a dand or huge wooden rod with fire emanating from all sides and hits Bahubali. Bahubali is buried up to his chest in the ground. When he emerges and retaliates, Bharata is immersed almost fully into the earth. Only his head remains above the ground. Bharata is now defeated. He cannot not face it.

Description of the war between Bharata and Bahubali

Elder brother, think, how unnecessarily
So many men are being killed
Is this why Rishabha incarnated
As the embodiment of truth and non-violence?

Is this why our revered father
Nurtured us under his loving gaze?
Will his joy be reflected
In this free flow of blood?

The whole society has been built on
The sweat of our father's efforts
To turn that into dry hay
Is reckless on our part

Our venerable father is assessing
The value of the life of a plant
We are making even the life of man
Equal to that of a grain of sand

Will blood be able to wash away
The stains it leaves behind?
Will any weapon be able to
destroy smouldering enmity?

When ego clashes with ego
There arises a heated cyclone
Then the eyes with sand blown into them
Begin to flower the seeds of suspicion

When will we, dear brother,
Be free from this bitterness of doubt?
To trample over people like this
How can it be called in anyway right?

Bharata

Younger brother, you are hundred per cent right!
Irrefutable is your speech
But only those words are valuable
Where action follows what you preach

Forget this lecturing session
Search out the path that is doable
On both sides the desire
to win has become foremost

To retreat now, brother, is impossible!
Righteousness has turned away, wealth and people destroyed
Will you be able to set this right?
Are you fully confident?

Bahubali

In the dictionary of Rishabha's sons
The word 'impossible' does not exist
Rain, send down showers to cleanse the land
Fertile and prosperous the earth will become

New thinking by Bharata-Bahubali

Desirous of victory we are
War is restricted to the two of us
Let the soldiers be only spectators
Then we might right the wrong

Duality means only war
One alone is beyond the dual
Enveloped in anger and greed, man
lives in duality, filled with fear

Victory, defeat, they go together
Duality is the game played by thought
In duality fight is inherent
Like oil which remains hidden in the sesame seed

A life lived in loneliness
Will not bring progress
May we search the middle path, such that
Violence does not breathe free

May the thinking of violent war change
Let us make a new beginning
Work ours will give the battlefield
A much desired new appearance

War will be non-violent from now
This is our firm resolve
We will engage in combat with our eyes,
resonating roar, fists and weapons, the order of four[1]

Call for cessation of war, soldiers
On both sides let there be such joy as
the first drop of rain delights the chatak bird
As the moon charms the chakor[2]

A common meeting ground has been found
Some great influence of the Lord
War will be fought between Bharata and Bahubali
Brothers, yet enemies. life is difficult to understand

Delighted was the army of the king of Bahali
Now definite is victory
Our king's arms are very strong
Unsuccessful will be the efforts of Bharata

Worried was the army of Emperor Bharata
Our master is of delicate build
Bahubali is strong in his limbs
In victory there is doubt

Reading the expressions on their faces
Which were clouded by doubt
In Bharata's face rose
A mixture of pride and manliness

The truth that words are not able to utter
Experience reveals instantaneously
Practice can be
the sole remedy

Obtaining instructions from the master Bharata
Once again life began to flow
In a trice the soldiers
constructed a long and deep trench, behold

Bharata himself got tied, a strong chain
around his arm, which the army had to pull
But like the bee which draws only the fragrance
Leaving the flower unmoved, the emperor could not be budged

When he lifted his arm to put his hand to his chest
The soldiers fell like nine pins, one atop the other
Just like in times of storm
Leaves fall off the tree together[3]

So doubts were thus clarified
And everyone's heart was filled with joy
The joy of victory
Will be beside our Lord's feet

To read the language of doubt
Is the first mark of a leader
The one who is able to assuage it
Becomes even greater

Dream-filled night, dream-filled sleep
One dream kept repeating itself
Victorious will be the king of ours
Sure like the flowing river in nature

Filled with eagerness and anticipation
Were all the three worlds of earth, heaven and hell
And the very first rays of the sun
Saw auspicious omens for the brothers

The battlefield into a meeting ground
has turned, this is without doubt
Raining is amity
Nowhere is there any enemy

Bahubali

O army chief, where is my
brother's place of residence?
Inform him that the younger brother is waiting
As one awaits the dawn

Tell the brother
Please remain free of fear
Elder is elder and younger is younger
This truth is universal

Why is he afraid, war this is not
Just a dialogue between brothers
He will surely remember the games
We have played at the feet of our father

After many days we will today meet
It will rain joy from the skies
All other pleasures are reflections
of the joy of the meeting of brothers

Of the great sutra of brothers' meeting
Who will do the true translation?

The coming of Bharata

Tearing the covering of the clouds
Shone a white flash across the skies
Removing the obstruction of distance
Came the elder brother crowned king

Embracing each other, exuberant minds
Not a glimpse of enmity or opposition
Both of them had got from the Lord
The sermon of right perspective

The one who lives in the memories of the past
Nourishes passion as it were
Denied he is of the right perspective
Only in friendship is there true happiness

Bahubali bowed and said,
Happiness on meeting my brother
That we should meet on the battlefield
That causes pain in my heart

If the elder was to come to Takshashila
What a grand welcome he would get
Brother elder, on this battle ground
Only the sinhanad is[4] heard

The land of Bahali is a land beautiful
Into this everyone can enter freely
Only the one who comes to attack is prohibited
And aggression is banned

Neither does the chakor meet the moon
Nor does the chatak get the first drop of rainwater
So too is the union of victory and defeat unheard
On a level playing ground

Come on brother! The moments of childhood
will come alive again
The autumn month has come to an end
See how beautiful is spring

War in the eyes

Having created a labyrinth of words
The younger brother looked at the elder
In Bharata's eyes there flashed
A powerful lightning

With the unblinking eyes[5] of the emperor
Light rays came flowing out
The eyes of Bahali however
Viewed it as a gift from the elder brother

The brothers had lived together
Each other's eyes they knew only too well
Today the language of knowing
Acquired a new interpretation

Both of them stood staring, eyes unblinking
and open, emitting light
Even for a second my Lord should not
see darkness thought the eyelids, as they kept open[6]

Days went past, no one won
Nor was anyone defeated
The power of keeping the gaze fixed is great
It can turn an ordinary man into a spiritual one

The Lord is finding it difficult
Thinking so the eyelids closed
As though before Bahubali
They bowed down in obeisance

The fixed gaze of the younger one
Announced the inevitable victory
In victory and defeat the witness are the eyelids
They have their own vocabulary

Brother, do not think
That by chance I have won
Will this child-like play be able to
decide the winner and the loser?

The deriding words of the king of Bahali
Attacked Bharata sharply
Vibrating with the inner voice, the heart
In the outside world expression found words

Bharata's sinhanad resounded
in all directions
The resonance was unparalleled
Of this there was no doubt

The earth trembled, the trees trembled
Even the celestial onlookers were in fear
Who will bring peace and grant fearlessness
Fear itself is beyond words

From reaction to action, from action
to reaction is the rule usual
That which manages man's mind
Is not thought but instant reflexes

All the directions were filled
With the roar of the king of Bahali
Bharata's roar in contrast was lost
As all elephants are before Airavata[7]

The cosmos cried victory is to Bahubali
Triumph is to the younger one
Bharata is the elder, but more powerful is the younger
The earth and sky are stunned

In the mind of the king of Bahali
A new enthusiasm sprouted
How will Bharata have confidence
in his own valour?

The vibrations of the sinhanad!
Is like the inner voice becoming eloquent
Sounds are similar expressions
Why are we grading them then?

The next challenge of muscle strength will
prove more meaningful
It will also be entertaining to watch
And to wrestle will give childish pleasure

The hands were brilliant
The feet touched the skies
The wondrous game of the two brothers
Filled the viewers with delight

Bharata elated with his own prowess
Saw the bright sky
Strong Bahubali's muscular arms
made the word 'impossible' seem absurd

Of meaning and disaster
The younger one analysed
In his two arms the emperor Bharata
He enveloped him and quelled the fight

In waste was the sleeping lion[8] awakened
In waste was there a passion for war
Why did I take the army chief's words
as the last word, repented Bharata

What success has victory brought?
The younger one is victorious
Definitely in the four stages of war
He will gain victory

Brothers! In the fist rests all the strength
See how powerful it is
It is stronger than even the mace
And tender as the blooming lotus

There is great power in the attack
May the fist fight begin
Said Bharata, this game is for young boys
Let there be no doubt of my victory

O great king, the power of words is always great
Who can measure its strength?
They can be sweet to the mind
As well as frightening as a forest

The younger one was spewing words
Bharata rose in raging passion great
One man's anguish creates
Sorrow in the other

Bharata then punched him cruelly
On his chest with his fist
The younger one got from the elder
Pain alone as gift

The earth and sky seemed to become one
Even the visible world became invisible
In this world of matching strength to strength
How can anyone be humble?

Coming back to consciousness
Bahubali then boxed him back
Bharata fell to the ground
Completely unconscious

It is not known why on the battlefield
Washed away are all relationships
With anger and aggression even
the man with eyes becomes blind

How can you be so heartless
Against my brother?
If you become devoid of love
How can you live with people?

Look after Bharata, reviving him is a must
Only then the conch of victory can sound
Hold the feather in your hand and fan him
for wind is the most potent of medicines in this world

Woke Bharata from a deep, unconscious state
How did the ochre dawn come?
Brother, why are you forgetting
The day has dawned spotless

The war with weapons yet remains
Come, let us both play
The victor will sit on the throne
Wearing a crown of thorns[9]

On one side, defeat
Would give birth to a feeling of shame
On the other side, the taunts
Would fester mental wounds

Picking up the ratna dand[10]
Bharata attacked with the speed of wind
The younger, broad-chested, long-armed one fell to the ground
As though night had descended on the day

The passion of rage is great
Seshnag came to the earth
Blooming was the lotus flower
In the environs light spread

Picking up the iron dand
Bahubali hit Bharata on the head
Trembling was the lap of the earth
Opened wide a pit deep as a lake

Bharata was now neck deep under the earth
Confounded was his side
Our Lord is getting destroyed
The king of Bahali will wear the crown

The army saw the head alone, the rest buried
under the ground
As though the branch alone stood without the trunk
The head seemed from the body removed

The body's strength, the mind's power
And the fiery web of anger
Manifested itself in Bharata's anguish
As he looked completely distraught

He was filled with rage
And with the humiliation of defeat
Light was covered with ash
Not visible any more was the divine personality

Right thinking, right decision
Is the divine gift of being sans passion
Only that person can get it
The one who has tasted sublimation.

Notes

1. Drishtiyudh, Shabdyudh, Mushtiyudh and Dandyudh.
2. The birds have been mentioned before and are favourite similies in Indian poetry. Chakor loves the moon, it is a case of unrequited love. The chatak remains thirsty for days just to get the first drop of rain.
3. The two verses, this one and the one above, refer to the incident where Bharata shows his army his strength.

4. Sinhanad is one of the ways in which war was fought. Five types of war had been mentioned: war through the eyes, through words, sounds, fist and the use of the rod.
5. The original word is animesh. This is a practice in which the eyes are not allowed to even blink. They are always kept open.
6. This is the beginning of drishtiyudh.
7. Airavata is Indra's vehicle and the most powerful white elephant.
8. Bahubali is being referred to as the sleeping lion.
9. The victor will be crowned king, but after killing his own brother. So his crown will feel like it is made of thorns.
10. Ratna dand has five branches embedded with gems and it can destroy all enemies and can fulfil all the wishes of the king. Through a special practice it can even funnel through 1,000 yojanas below the earth.

Canto XVIII

Bharata is bewildered. He, the chakravarti, the emperor, has lost it all. Desperation runs through his entire body—this cannot be allowed to happen.

Even though he has decided never to use the weapons and the treasures he has, his defeat weakens that resolve and he picks up the chakr and sends it against Bahubali. Now victory is definite, he thinks. It is a very potent chakr that not only emanates fire but can destroy anyone. Bahubali stands and watches the chakr coming towards him.

Instead of hurting him the chakr circumambulates him and returns to Bharata. Bharata is shocked with the chakr's action.

Bahubali is enraged that Bharata has transgressed the rules. He also feels this is no brother but an enemy. He raises his clenched hammer to beat his brother into the ground, when he hears a word of caution from the celestials. The brother has lost, you have won, drop your anger. What he did was wrong, but why should you wrong too? Bahubali sees wisdom in this advice, and the fist that had risen to kill now reaches his own head and plucks out the hair in preparation to become a monk.

Bharata is shocked as he watches Bahubali. Instead of attacking he has made a sacrifice. Where there is sacrifice there is victory, peace and happiness. Bahubali's sacrifice is an antidote to the ego—it signals the movement from war to peace, from victory to greater victory.

Bahubali stands in meditation unmindful of time and space. Creepers grow on him and birds make their nests. Then Bhagwan Rishabha sends Brahmi and Sundari to find him and bring him to their fold. What had been stopping Bahubali was his reluctance to be junior to his brothers if he joins the fold. But Brahmi and Sundari tells him that there is no concept of junior or senior, each one reigns in his kingdom. Humility is the key to moksha.

Bharata salutes Bahubali and returns to Ayodhya. He gives Bahubali's kingdom to his son Chandrayasha, then comes back to his own kingdom and reflects on his material surroundings and the choices made by his brothers.

Bharata is in his bath when his ring falls off his finger and he finds that his hands are actually not so nice to look at. Wearing it on again, he realizes he is trying to make them look attractive. That is his moment of insight, when he understands all beauty is external and impermanent. All that is permanent is the beauty of the soul.

The veetaraga rasa finds home in Bharata too. He too joins the fold. The story ends with Rishabha's nirvana.

The swami or Rishabha had been the sun in the people's lives—he had given them inner light and showed them the path to purity. He is now gone. The poem asks: who will be the next spiritual leader? This is in keeping with the beauty of Jain philosophy which believes this world has no beginning, no end …

Bharata's ire

Two branches of one tree
Each with its own experience
Heat is the nature of the sun
The moon is of cool temperament

'You are the younger brother
And so I will pardon your mistake
I don't know how pardon will be
Accepted by the chakra,' said Bharata

The total defeat stoked
A scorching fire inside
Stirred by that the elder is
speaking valiant words of defeat

How can even the wise think
When possessed by anger?
Breaking the order, how can man
follow and respect discipline?

Raging with anger, Bharata threw
the chakra at the younger brother
Fear gripped everyone—the evil and the divine
Chaos reigned on earth

So many doubts and hopes!
So many thoughts and counter-thoughts!
Will this piece of iron
be able to vanquish Bahubali's courage?

However strong man is
His body is after bones and flesh
In the face of divine power, how long
can the wick draw oil for sustenance?

People hovered between belief and disbelief
Their agitation was now past hearing
In the meanwhile, the eyes saw
something that was way beyond thought

Circumambulating Bahali in all humility
All around the king of Bahali it went
And atop his right arm, on his shoulder came to rest
The play of destiny is beyond words

Bharata's mind was plagued by doubt
Who is emperor, me or Bahubali?
Till today I have nourished illusions
Today truth has got its place

If I am emperor, how then in the younger brother's
hand the chakra has seated itself?
That which I thought was milk
Turns out to be water filled with whey

The chain of doubts and possibilities
In one second multiplied
Like the farmer sees with wonder
How the sapling overnight became a tree

Now what will happen? The younger one
will send the chakra on Bharata
The future waits unknown, like a story untold
While the meaning of war remains a massacre of men

The chakra then flew through the sky
Agitation amongst the people grew chaotic
How will this fight between brothers
be ever resolved?

Came the foaming waves of chaos
Humble, like the obedient student, bowing, circumambulating,
to Bharata's arm it returned
The ignorant, plagued by doubt, said the chakra is supernatural

Bharata was relieved to see the return of the chakri
Its humility told him he had nothing to fear
His face was joyous like the bamboo flower
Which blooms amidst dark and fearsome thunderstorm

Bharata had transgressed rules, the chakr
was not part of the four modes of war
With the disrespect to decorum rose Bahubali's indignation
And blinding anger snapped brotherly ties

The hands rose and with fists that were clenched
He ran towards Emperor Bharata
Anger began dripping from his being
Fear spread on all sides

How will the chakra or the chakri[1]
be able to escape today?
The great and revered Ikshvaku race
How will its pride be safeguarded?

At that moment the celestial beings
Stopped Bahubali on his path
Move away from my path, he thundered
Do you have the desire to die?

We will not die, immortal we are
We have a message from the immortals themselves
Nurtured and nourished you have been with truth like nectar
Then why this destroying rage?

Peace peace, calm down
The proud inheritor of the Rishabha line
Desirous of pearls are
The swans of Manasarovar[2]

With a few drops of water sprinkled on the milk
The rising froth of the boil settled down
With great difficulty anger was put to rest
And energized were peaceful thoughts

Alas! Alas! Rage is the creator
of the determination to war
Of infighting between brothers
This is the seed, this the root

Mind changed, thoughts changed
The whole world changed
We have heard from the revered father
That sacrifice is the essence of best life[3]

End of war

To which rhythm
is this verse moving forward?
The eyes carrying questions
Saw only one reflection

Drawn across the dark
Clouds of the mind was a sketch
In the second phase came peace
The first was filled with painful war

What happened that giving up the battlefield
Bahubali is walking away?
Are vibrating messages
Coming all the way from Rishabha?
Even the sky is vibrating
And sounds fill the air
To which meter and rhythm
are the feet moving forward?

The flow of questions began
The wave of imagination came along
Silent answer in the shimmer
of the winter's moonlight
Unmoving and as determined as the Himalayas
The inclination towards renunciation
To which meter and rhythm
are the feet moving forward?

Wearing the garland of victory
Why is he deserting the battlefield?
Wearing he is the crown of fearlessness
Then why is he feeding on fear?
Incomprehensible is the riddle
This is the veil over truth
To which meter and rhythm
are the feet moving forward?

In a vacuum rose a chorus of voices,
Sacrifice alone can solve the war

This fire can be quenched
only by the water of sacrifice
The poison of egotism is spread in this world
Sacrifice is indeed the only drop of ambrosia
To which meter and rhythm
are the feet moving forward?

Silent is speech, body still
Both the hands hanging down to the knees
Standing in the stance of meditation
Bahubali looks a realized monk
Bowing Bharata said,
Here begins a new chapter of peace
To which meter and rhythm
are the feet moving forward

Indeed, fault is mine
War I have waged with my brother
Taking the boon of victory
Standing he is like the Himalayas
O Ocean of forgiveness, forgive!
Now forgiveness alone is the answer
To which meter and rhythm
are the feet moving forward?

The words uttered were as though unheard
Meditation unstinted, stable the mind
The dialogue of silence sweet
Even the body became bodyless
With strong faith
Rare moment of light this is
To which meter and rhythm
are the feet moving forward?

Returned the emperor
The war ground is now a field of peace
To claim the rights over Bahali
Chandrayasha[4] was successful
Now towards Vinita
Bharata is going back
To which meter and rhythm
are the feet moving forward?

Kayotsarga by Bahubali

Ego and arrogance are two soldiers who
strengthen the desire for kingship, whimsical as it is
They together have written the entire history of the world
Who has escaped the intoxication of their madness?

How do I go in the presence of the Lord?
Some things are known and some unknown in the script of fate
How will I bow to my younger brothers?
If I do not, I will transgress the discipline of the fold

Practice of restraint is the only secret of being a monk
And the solitude of the forest is ideal for that
So what if I am physically far, mentally I am close
After all, every one cannot be close to victory[5]

Through restraint alone can one be a monk
Solitude of the forest is the best
Even though the Lord may be far away physically
Mentally he is nigh

Stopped the feet that were to move forward
Rooted were the clouds which were ascending to the sky
To the restless body kayotsarga gives stillness
To live within oneself is the greatest strength

The path to moksha is one plagued by doubt
A sterling example is Bahubali
One who decides amidst confusion and action is a man
One who decides away from discussion, in stillness, is a pillar
of strength

Stillness gave Bahubali spiritual elevation
Creepers made his arms and legs their support
The whole body as though was covered in greenery
And the hair on his head looked like saffron fields

On his shoulder birds made their nests
The cuckoo sung melodiously
The sky and earth saw an amazing sight
Some new pole star has come to the horizon

Continuously does the cycle of time keep moving
Like the beautiful parijat blooms only in a peaceful forest
The consciousness lives only in a city free of ego
In one who is able to see himself within himself[6]

Sermon by Rishabha

O Brahmi! O Sundari! See your brother
is stuck on the banks and the tide is high[7]
For over a year now he has been following the vow of restraint
Entitled thus he is for realization

The door is closed,[8] go both of you to open it
Evaluate your brother with love maternal
Forgetting the soul, body he has become
Matter has with matter attracted

They arrived at the specified place
Seen is not the brother anywhere
But Lord Rishabha would not have spoken thus
Definitely in some corner of the forest he must be hidden

Man has searched for truth that is concealed
Through suggestion the clues have been laid out
But what has this human body been able to conceal
Was revealed by the aura glowing above and around it

The rays of light wove a net unique
As though the sun had decorated the courtyard of the home
The two sisters saw with unblinking eyes
Lightning flashing across the sky

This is not a tree but a person definitely
This is not someone commonplace but worth revering
The brilliant aura announces he is Rishabha's son
In the form of a tree he is a radiant man

Standing near and in front of him they said
O Bahubali, why are you wearing a monk's garb?
See brother, see with the two eyes
On the scale of existence measure your soul

Grateful we are to the Lord for being able to see the soul
All souls are equal and enchanting in their equanimity
To bow in greeting is social conduct, in truth we all are equal
Why then is the creeper of arrogance growing in your heart?

Brother, descend! Descend from the elephant![9]
Then you will experience and feel the soil of the land
The elephant rider cannot reach the presence of Adinatha
Lord Adinatha is the proponent of equality

This arrogance, brother, has blocked your way
In this sea of emotions, humility is the only boat
Can a stone ever swim across the waters?
Or will barren land ever be able to grow grapes?

Now why don't you open up brothers?
Lend me your eyes and ears, your sisters two are speaking
Our speech is the voice of awakening
Consciousness is indestructible, arrogance fleeting

Vibrating with the resonance of the soul was the entire earth
The inner being of the monk was throbbing in that vibration
This voice that seems recognizable—from where is it coming?
Who is giving me the directions to the unknown destination?

Have the nuns Brahmi and Sundari come?
Have they brought a message from Adinatha?
How the creepers have made me their support
See how the birds have made their nest

I am mobile, how have I then become rooted?
I am the soul, then how did I become pillar-like?
I created the illusion of stillness within me
But how did my flesh becomes so scaled with dust?

I belong to that world in which there is no stagnation
I belong to that world in which there is no ego
The vision of the soul is the first that one gets to behold
Arrogance does not come as an obstruction along this path

Pure and even purer stream of results
Pure incandescence saw the shore nearby
As the feet rose to meet the Lord
The shadow of the cloud became the umbrella

To behold the soul is to behold Adinatha
He saw his wife in person, his home
All of them together came into his vision
In the month of Chaitra all the flowers bloomed
Now the feet moved forward and to the Lord's presence went
How much there is to know in the unknown

Bharata

Auspicious recitations of holy men
First sign of awakening
Lord arise, give up sleep
Auspicious is the entire surrounding

First moment, first thought
gives some idea
In Bharata's mind there arose today
a new picture, a beautiful heaven

Neither father, nor brother
Nor even the wife here
Bharata alone is king
What kind of kingdom is this?

One day in that home environment
Used to live the entire family

Now Bharata is alone
Amazing is the way of life

In truth every man is alone
Society is solely for transactions
Forgotten have I the transcendental perspective[10]
The gross has become the essence of life

There is no river whose
waters are immobile
So too in this world of temporary residence
Who will write the history of continuity?

Every corner of the mind was filled
With the understanding of impermanence
They were the first rays of sunshine
That lit the inner being

The state of delusion was shaken up
Awoken was inner wisdom
The staircase to detachment built
Distanced were all obstructions

Reached he in bliss the lotus feet of Adinatha
Those seconds when the brothers met
Were so beautiful that the sky
wrote a story of never-ending beauty

Lord! My brothers have entered
the kingdom of the soul
I alone lived so long
In a world of materialism

When will they become a full hundred?
When will I be initiated?
When will I behold my soul?
When will my being radiate light?

Questions these are not
It is my eloquent anguish, O Lord!
That I find the water to quench this fire
Give me such a blessing, O Lord!

Rishabha

You have a soul, Bharata
Then why are you sad?
Even though it lives in a huge ocean
The fish is still thirsty

The strong penance to build detachment
May it increase like the waning moon
Remain like the lotus on the water surface
And like the sun in constant movement

Gaining the mantra for a new lifestyle
Changed was the mind
When the heart changes, life's direction changes
Nature changes by itself

Returned the emperor back to Ayodhya
His inner being was lit up
First he lived in the royal palace
Now in the soul he resides

On the throne of detachment
The emperor seated himself
Sitting on this throne even the
old is, look, all anew again

The path is the same, the palace the same
The very same enchanting harem
The same food, the same drinks
The same arch of experiences

Everything was the same, the same festivals
Only the same perspective was not there
Changed was the perception of matter
No problems arising from the material

On a dry wall, dry dust
never catches on
On the mental plane of Bharata
There remained no blemish of sorrow

Ages passed, years passed
Time has its own cycle
Some things in this world are dispensable
Some things however are a must

Came one jewel-like moment
When engrossed in his bath was Bharata
There suddenly were
vibrations everywhere

Fell the ring from the ring finger
Where has its beauty gone?
The bath became the shelter
of thought, in loss came wealth

He wore again the ornament on the finger
Its beauty increased and so did the field of thought
That which the intellect can see
The eyes are not able to

Removed again, put on again
He saw truth personified
Decorating the body with more matter
Body too is matter after all

I am the soul and in the soul
will be my unmoving residence
The experience of the soul is unparalleled
Beautiful and enthralling

With the transparency of a palace of glass
Matched the purity of the heart
In the moment of purity
Man becomes free of all ills

It is natural to value light
Can the reflection be without value?
Everything has its own glory
Bitter and yet the neem is beneficial

The king is seeing the mirror
And was looking at himself
As he kept looking he saw
the light of a supreme being

He has seen the soul
He was become realized
His penance has borne fruit naturally
The gift of detachment

Distanced was he from his kingdom
He no longer was the people's emperor
All the limits that bound him have broken
Free and larger than life he has emerged

Neither with Ayodhya, nor with the palace
remains any bondage
Awoken is the monk within
All ties only with the soul

The first generation gave to the next
All its worldly treasures
The number of one hundred was now complete
In Rishabha's presence he found new joy

Nirvana of Rishabha

From the shore of death
The other side was visible
Now bodyless is the one who lived in the body
Free—freedom from attachment

The land where he stood was now famous
Known to the world as the sacred land
Brilliant ochre spread across the sky
A new sun rose giving way to a new dawn

Six days of fasting unstinted
And stillness of the body defined a new measure
of creation in the mudra of paryankasan[11]
The realized Lord became liberated and at peace

Bharata was present, Indra was present
And was present the entire fold of monks
All the members of the laity were watching
In a second the pulsating body came to rest

Embodied existence is transient
All coalesced forms will dissolve
The swami has attained nirvana
Now, whence will the sun illumine our lives?

Notes

1. Chakr is the weapon, its master is the chakri or the emperor.
2. It is believed that the swans in the lake of Manasarovar in the Himalayas eat only pearls. In this context it means Bahubali should aspire only for the best course of action.
3. Mythology says the fist Bahubali raised, he never lowered. He took it straight to his head and pulled out a clump of hair. This, perhaps, prompts the refrain in the next few verses where the poet asks which direction is Bahubali headed towards now.
4. Chandrayasha was Bahubali's son. Bharata gave him his father's kingdom to rule.
5. The victor wears a vermilion mark on the forehead. So the poet says every brow cannot be close to the mark, similarly it need not be close to Rishabha. The meaning has been retained in the translation of these two lines.
6. Parijat is the name of the flower Nyctanthes arbor-tristis. By seeing himself within himself means seeing the soul within.
7. He is not able to cross over. The need to cross a ford or river to get to the other side, the spiritual side or divine side, is an oft used simile in Indian literature.
8. The door to moksha.
9. The elephant represents the ego and the one who still has his ego cannot reach Adinatha, the first Lord (Bhagwan Rishabha).
10. Nischay nay (the transcendental perspective) helps to know subtle truths while vyavahara nay (the pragmatic perspective) helps to know gross truths.
11. Paryankasan is a yogic posture called the bed pose: the legs are folded in under the buttocks and the arms are stretched behind.

EPILOGUE

Truth is not just
What I believe it is
The sky is not just
What I see it as
This infinite, do not
limit within your home
But in your home too
there is the sky, accept this truth

The birth of Rishabha
A symbol of progress and peace
Drawing the Age of Twins
Into a social structure and laying the base
The forest dweller, town dweller became
Buildings multiplied
The family unit came into being
Relationships acquired meaning

The field of agriculture was thrown open
And other vocations were defined

From ownership was born the idea of security
And weaponry came as guarantee
A new experience was being gained
Of reading-writing in education
Action as though prevailed upon organized inaction

In the newborn conception of a kingdom
Enthusiasm was like that of a child's
Foremost quality was that of self-discipline
Intrinsic nature dictated everything
There was simplicity and modesty
Anger and greed were under control
Anger and greed lost in tranquility
The story of administration
Was naturally one of peace

Simple king, simple subjects
Simple administration
Over the entire sky and earth
Was spread the mantra of simplicity
Strife, representations, dispute
were all hitherto unknown
Few desires, little property
Everyone was a natural master

Healthy body, healthy mind
The emotions were so pure
No teaching of sacred texts, nor
Were authors of scriptures well-known
Close to nature was the way of life
Skills were developed next to naught
In the experience of each breath
Faith found expression

A teaching of the soul was gained
Self-discipline was successful
Even in the dearth of material objects
Society was content
To experience satisfaction is joy
Sorrow is extreme discontent
Thinking born of contentment
Is always faultless

Mental power gives power and prosperity
Is the cause of arrogance
The two together a formidable pair make
And work constantly to create emotional turmoil
The invisible dharma empowers
One with courage

Power is the mind's, and prosperity
is the cause of arrogance
The pair together is active
And work an emotional turmoil
Dharma invisible, empowered
it is with courage
The one who equality does not know
Is far from the path of moksha

In following the guru's teachings
Lies the knowledge of learning
In following the path of humility
Lies the secret of true success
The essence of Rishabha's life story
Is in the knowing of the soul
At the core is the house of the soul
And along its periphery lies the world.

AFTERWORD

Even though the story is mythological, Rishabhayan has been told to highlight the fundamental principles of Jainism. Acharya Mahapragya edited the *Agamas* and rendered them into Hindi from Prakrit. Many ideas held within Rishabhayan are based on them. Other mythological renderings are *Sambodhi*, which tells the story of Meghakumar and Asruveena which is the story of Mahavira. *Jain Darshan, Manan aur Mimamsa* is another work of Acharya Mahapragya's in Hindi which contains much of the background material, with more emphasis on the teachings. Specifically, additional information which has helped in the translation of the work has been from *Trisastishlakapurush* in addition to the *Uttaradhyayana sutra*, the *Suyagado* and *Tanam*, not to mention the *Tatvartha sutra* which holds much of the idea of anekanta. Acharya Mahapragya has himself written several books on anekanta in order to demystify the premise on which Jainism is built: the idea that truth is multi-dimensional and contradictory elements can live together.

The story ends as though in wait for the next Tirthankara, in keeping with the philosophy of a beginning-less beginning and an endless end, with emphasis on the element of continuity of life. There were twenty-three Tirthankaras after Rishabha in our time cycle. Mythology gave way to include some history with the twenty-second Tirthankara, Prasvannatha. The teachings of the twenty-fourth Tirthankara, Vardhamana Mahavira, is well documented and his life detailed not just in Jain texts but also in Buddhist scriptures. Much of this has formed the corpus of Jain teachings available today.